SECRET CROMER & SHERINGHAM

Lorna Talbott

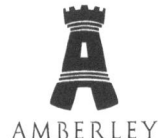

AMBERLEY

First published 2019

Amberley Publishing
The Hill, Stroud
Gloucestershire, GL5 4EP

www.amberley-books.com

ISBN 978 1 4456 9004 9 (print)
ISBN 978 1 4456 9005 6 (ebook)

British Library Cataloguing in Publication Data.
A catalogue record for this book is available from the
British Library.

Origination by Amberley Publishing.
Printed in Great Britain.

Appointed GPSR EU Representative: Easy Access
System Europe Oü, 16879218
Address: Mustamäe tee 50, 10621, Tallinn, Estonia
Contact Details: gpsr.requests@easproject.com, +358
40 500 3575

Contents

Introduction

The term secret can be interpreted by different people in different ways. A secret to one person can be an obvious fact to another. This book reveals the things that, after over half a century of happy holidays in the Cromer and Sheringham area, I realised that I still didn't know! The history of the pier and the fact that the first one was constructed in the fourteenth century, how the two towns have been affected by many wars and the church that lies under the sea beyond the pier are just some of the things that I have learned. *The Hound of the Baskervilles* was inspired by the region and a king played golf on the cliffs. Flint rocks and fossils are just a part of the amazing geology that I have discovered and there is a mermaid in one of the churches in Sheringham.

My own favourite secret, however, is the Sheringham Shoal. This great expanse of eighty-eight wind turbines, which are 15 miles out to sea, opened in 2012 after three years of construction. The turbines are 262 feet tall and their blades are 170 feet long. Each year, the Shoal produces enough energy to power around a quarter of a million homes.

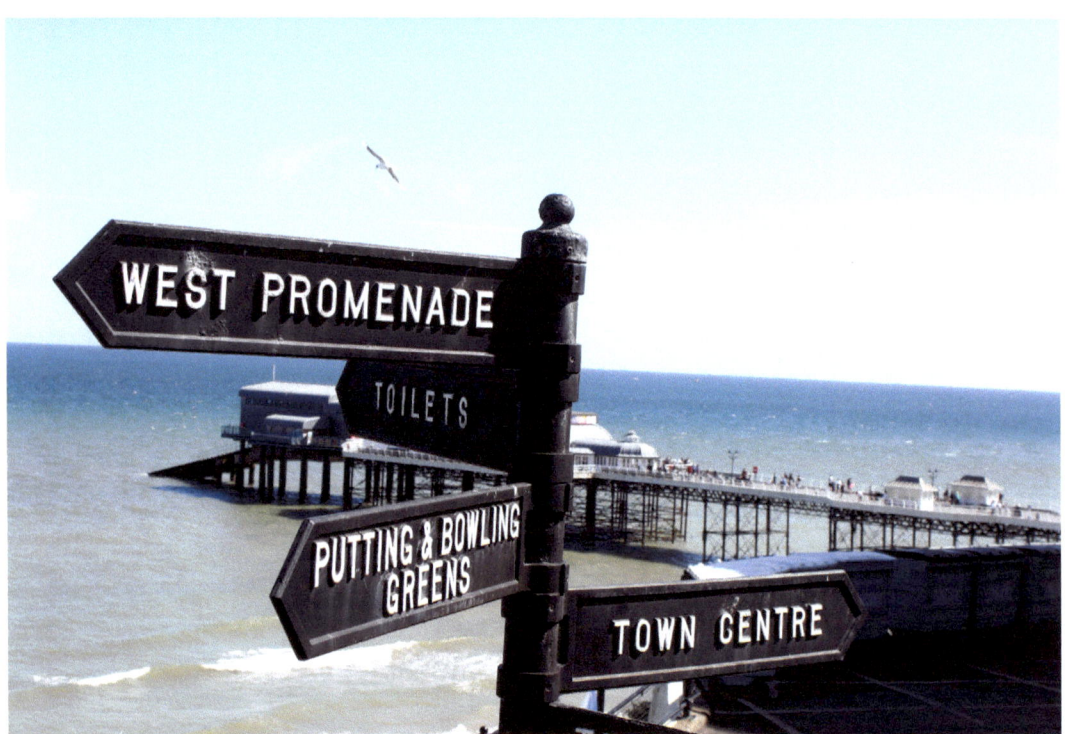

A signpost in Cromer points to happy holidays and history.

This completely environmentally friendly energy is created when the wind, which blows quite consistently that distance out to sea, turns the blades. The blades, in turn, work a turbine, which a generator then converts to electrical current. Each of the two substations that accompany the wind farm have 25-mile-long cables to export the electricity to the mainland and then to the National Grid. The Sheringham Shoal is an excellent ecological project but why is it a secret to me?

Because the Sheringham Shoal hides. Sometimes I look out to sea from the promenade at either Cromer or Sheringham and all I see is sea, even when the weather appears clear. Sometimes I look out to sea and I am amazed at how large and close the Sheringham Shoal looks, and I wonder why I didn't see them last time. I am assured that it is just sea mist that obscures them from time to time, and that they can, in fact, be seen on 60 per cent of occasions. I prefer to think that the turbines like to play hide and seek with me and anyone else enjoying the view, and they all run further out to sea where they cannot be seen from the shore.

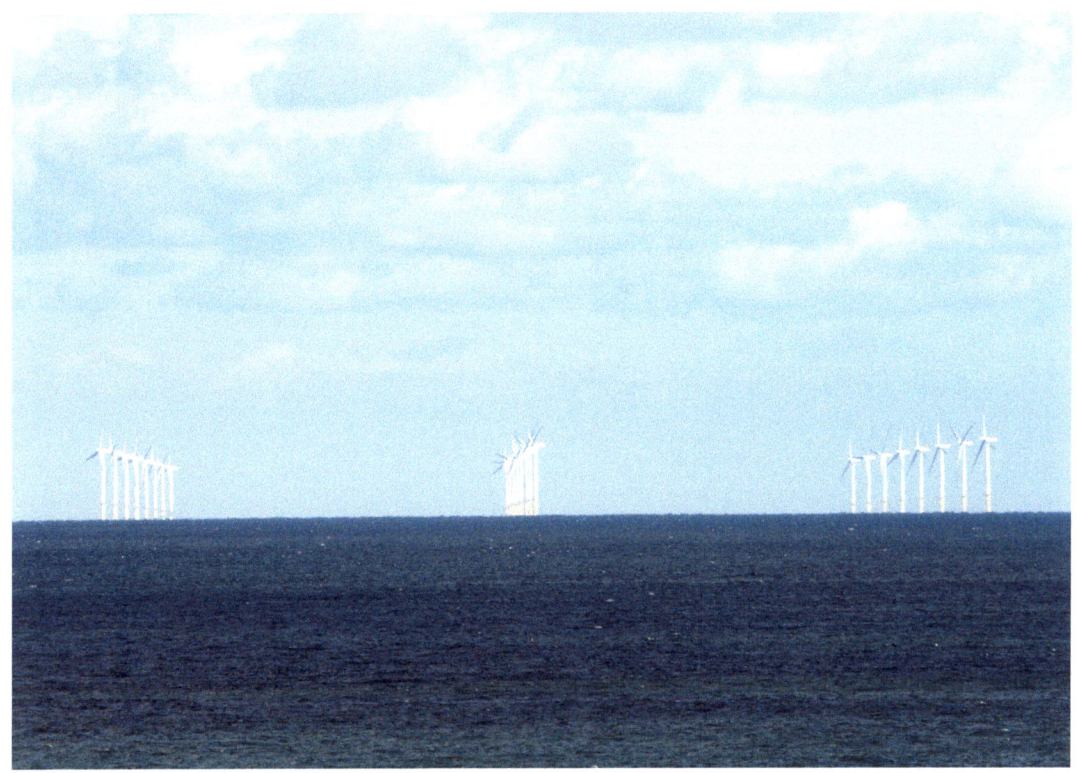

Sheringham Shoal wind farm on a clear day.

1. Origins Uncovered

Cromer and Sheringham are two well-loved seaside resorts and exploring their past reveals history going back millennia. Modern Cromer and Sheringham are barely recognisable now as the settlements that used to stand on the sites when they were listed under other names in the Domesday Book.

Cromer is called 'The Gem of the Norfolk Coast' and the town motto of Sheringham, when translated, means, 'The sea enriches and the pine adorns'. These honorary titles are both quite recent additions to the towns but it is surprising just how apt these mottos are. Looking at the pre-historic origins of this part of the British coastline it seems the history of the area does surprisingly involve gems, ancient pine forests and the unavoidable influence of the sea.

The fragile, sedimentary cliffs that make up the coastline in this part of Norfolk were created around a hundred thousand years ago. Chalk deposits up to 1,200 feet deep were created when the remains of millions of tiny sea shells were gradually compressed. These

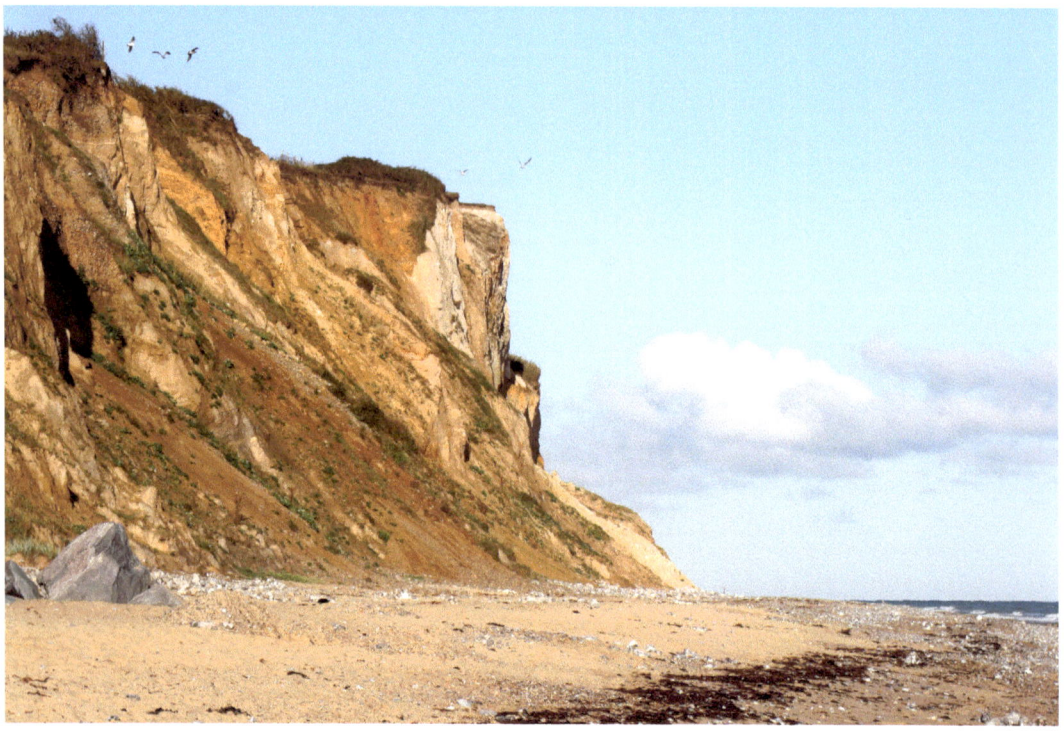

An abundance of fossils hide in the chalk-layered cliffs.

chalk layers hold within them other strata and one of these is the Forest Bed. This layer can be seen at the base of the cliffs near Cromer and Sheringham and was named in the belief that it was the remains of an ancient pine forest. Many tree trunks were found in this bed, but it is now thought to be the mouth of one of the great rivers that coursed through the land mass of Europe at that time. The river picked up a lot of tree wreckage and other debris on its journey and this accumulated into layers as it surged into the sea.

The cliffs at West Runton, which is between Sheringham and Cromer, are particularly rich in fossils. The fragility of the cliff and the importance of the site scientifically prevents any digging, but crumbling chalk, land slips and high tides expose new finds constantly. Sheringham museum houses some of these fossils including the leg bone of a mammoth. However, a more exciting find was made in these cliffs in 1990 when an 85 per cent complete skeleton of an elephant, a Steppe mammoth from 600,000 years ago, was excavated here. It is renowned for being the largest, oldest and most complete elephant skeleton ever found. The immense size of the fossil means it cannot be locally exhibited in its entirety, but Cromer museum has part of this exciting set of remains on show.

DID YOU KNOW?
During prehistoric times Great Britain was just a small part of a massive landmass or 'supercontinent' and was completely landlocked. In the Palaeozoic era, standing where the seafront of Cromer or Sheringham now are, and looking due north, would reveal thousands of miles of land stretching ahead. Over time, the land moved and broke up to form the continents we know today. Now, there is nothing at all but sea between Sheringham and Cromer promenades and the Arctic Circle.

Another abundant content of the chalk layers is flint, which is a form of the gemstone quartz. Flint has a rounded, nodular form and the nodules are found on the beaches as they break away from the cliff. The distinctive shape is due to the way it was formed. The ancient seabeds contained the burrows of large molluscs. The empty burrows became filled with remains of prehistoric vegetation and marine animals, which then became petrified and formed flint. A specific formation of flint is unique to the Cromer and Sheringham area and this has the local name of 'Pot Stones'. These are large, ring-shaped flint rocks and are actually called paramoudra. They can be seen on the sandy beaches, especially when the tide is out.

Flint is easily broken into flakes and was used to make sharp-edged tools by prehistoric man. This led to early man settling in the area where the valuable material was found. The nodules were also collected and used with mortar for building homesteads. This use for flint in building local cottages has continued.

The area was continuously populated, but the first written record of either town only occurs in the Domesday Book of 1086. Although Cromer and Sheringham are not mentioned in the Domesday Book by name, they are listed under the names by which

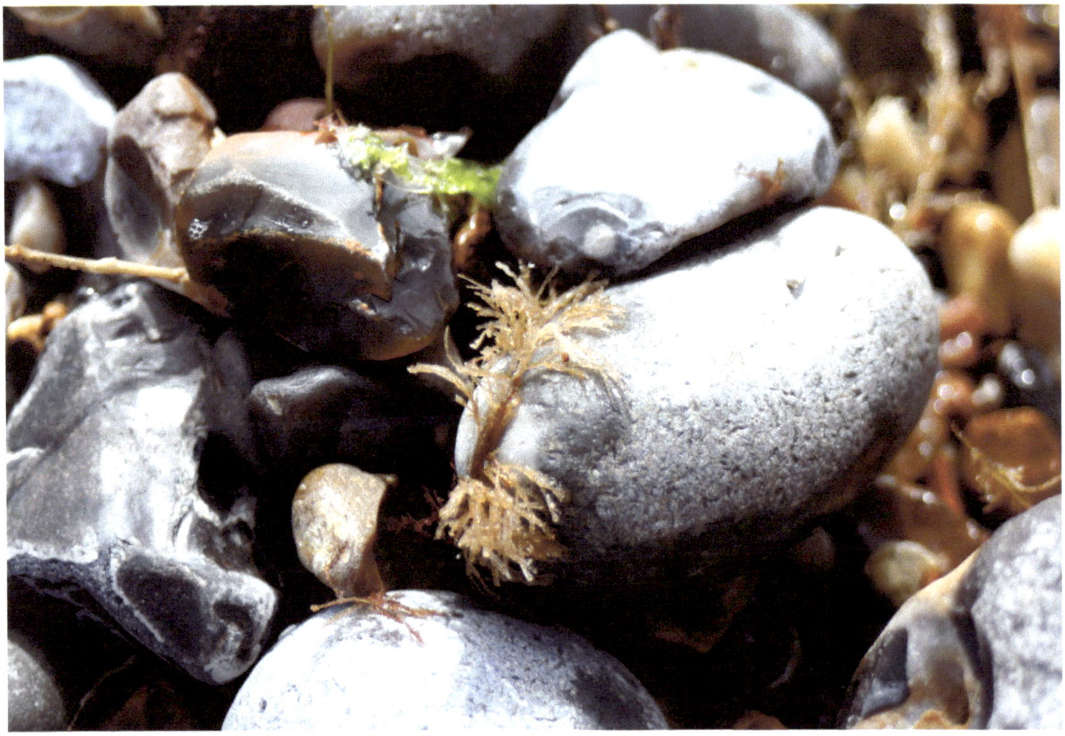

The numerous flint pebbles are both beautiful and practical.

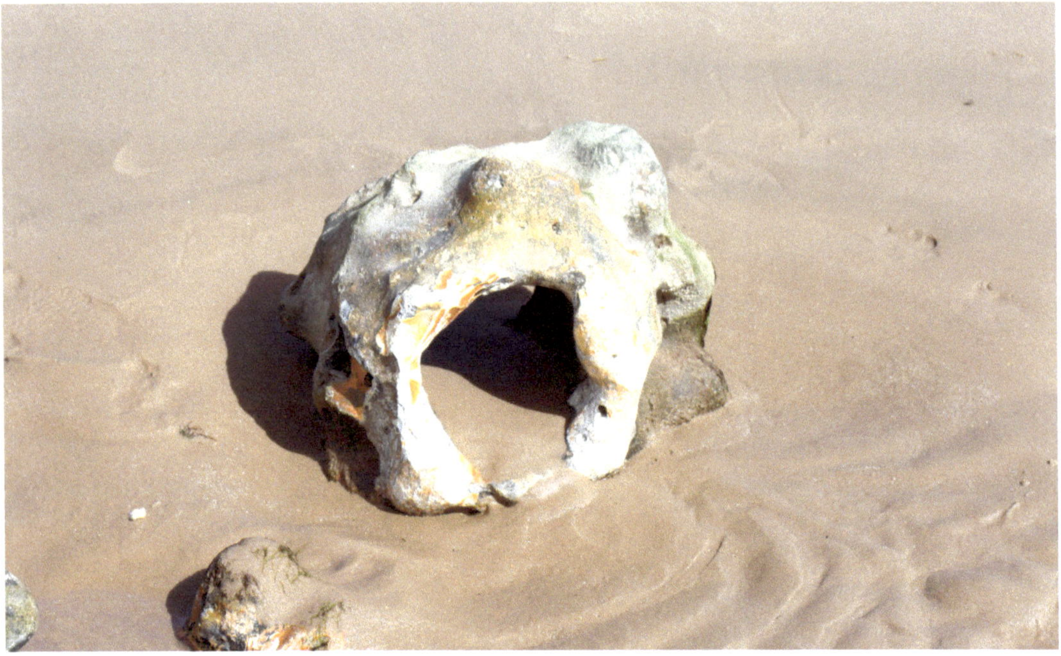

Large ring-shaped paramoudra are unique to the area.

they were previously known. The village of Shipden, which became Cromer, is recorded as having seventeen households that were taxable at 1.9 geld units. The larger settlement of Silingham, which changed its name to Sheringham, had twenty-eight households and a church, taxable to 3.2 geld units.

DID YOU KNOW?
The church that had served the old town of Shipden Juxta Mare slipped, with the town, into the sea. The ruin became known as Church Rock. The bricks broke down over the years but remains of the church could still be seen at low tides. However, in 1888, a steamer struck the remains. Although no lives were lost, it was considered prudent to blow up Church Rock to ensure it was no longer a danger to shipping. Remains of church masonry are still on the seabed and people claim they can often hear the bells.

The name Shipden is derived from 'sheep den'. Originally, there were two villages adjacent to each other: Shipden Juxta Mare and Shipden Juxta Felbrigg. Unfortunately, Shipden Juxta mare, which means 'sheep fold by sea', proved to be far too close to the sea, and was washed away in storm surges in the fourteenth century. The other village of Shipden continued to thrive and went on to have the prefix of Crowemere, meaning 'a gap in the cliffs'. However, by the fifteenth century all mention of Shipden disappeared and from being known by the long title of 'the gap in the cliffs with a sheep fold' the simple name of Cromer evolved for the village.

The name Silingham means 'home of Sciras people', and over time the name got corrupted through both Siringham and Schyringham to become Sheringham. A small fishing settlement, in medieval times the fishermen and their families lived a distance away from the sea, in the area now known as Upper Sheringham. Their boats were in an anchorage close to the shoreline and reached through a gap in the cliffs. Any equipment was left in huts nearby. The fishermen gradually built homes to incorporate their huts and moved closer to the sea where they could fish more conveniently. This new fishing area became Lower Sheringham. Upper Sheringham was populated by merchants and farmers and as each increased in size, the two villages gradually merged to create the larger town of Sheringham.

Although the sea was vital to the economic prosperity of Cromer and Sheringham, it was also a constant danger. In the fourteenth century, the village of Shipden Juxta Mare had only recently been washed into the sea making navigation near the shoreline treacherous. The first pier in Cromer was built in 1390 as a means to make it safer for any boats trying to land. At Sheringham a small enclosed harbour had been constructed for similar safety reasons but it was soon apparent that this caused silting up of the sea channels used by the towns fishermen when bringing their boats in to land. The harbour was eventually replaced with jetties. It was soon noticed that the pier and jetties helped to

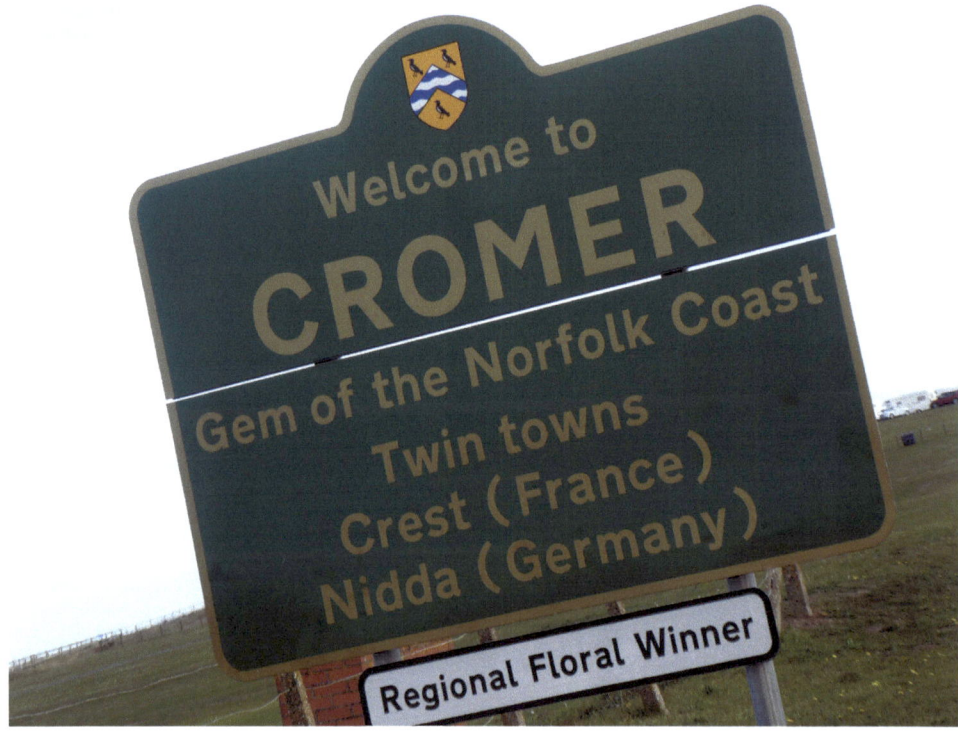

Cromer was once one half of twin villages called Shipden.

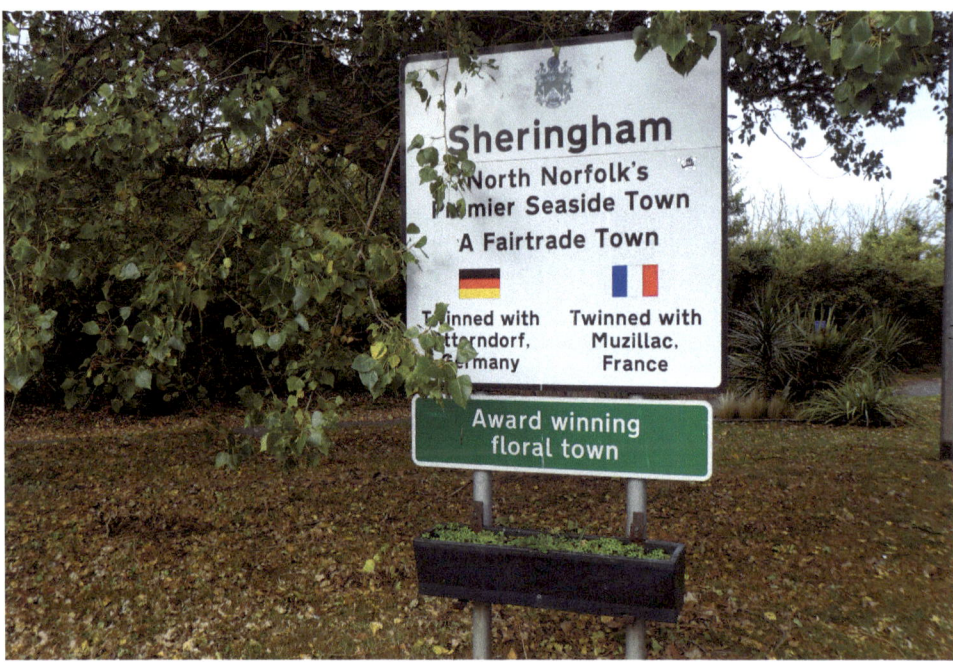

Sheringham fishermen began a new village nearer to the sea.

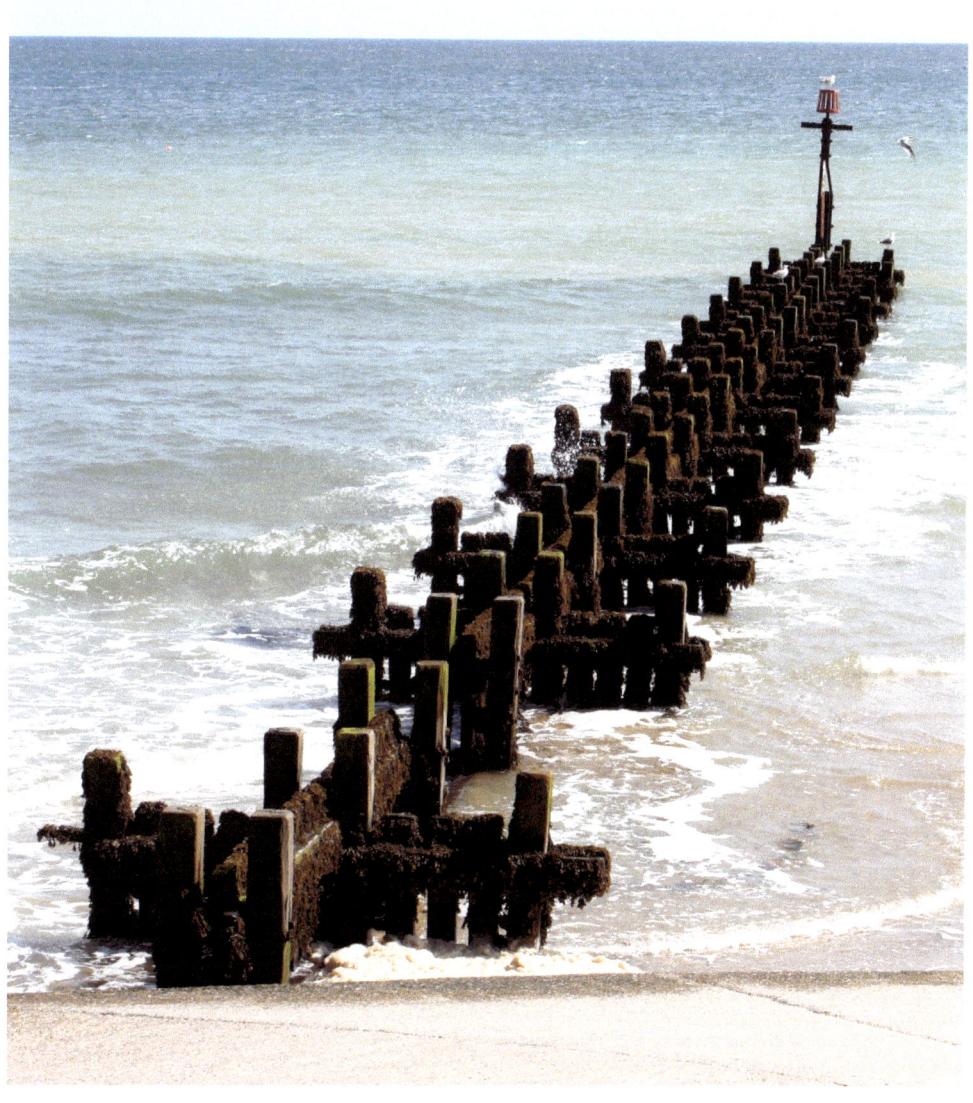

Weathered wooden groynes help to prevent erosion by the sea.

prevent erosion, or as noted in a report, 'The swallowing up and drowning of a great many houses'. This observation was the beginning of sea defences and the wooden groynes that line the beach have been a familiar sight ever since.

Cromer and Sheringham are fortunate nearby villages like Eccles, Foulness, Overstrand and Sidestrand have all been lost in full or part to the sea, despite the planting of coarse Marram grass in an attempt to stabilise the sandy and friable cliff edge. Marram grass grows on sand dunes and the root system helps to keep the sand together and prevent weather erosion. This works further inland but the grass cannot prevent damage caused by the ferocity of the sea.

Apart from the street layout none of the medieval features of either Cromer and Sheringham remain. The houses have been replaced over time and now both towns are very much of nineteenth-century origin with more recent additions. The exceptions are the parish church in Cromer and All Saints Church in Upper Sheringham, which date from the fourteenth century. Many of the houses in Cromer and Sheringham have now become rental accommodation for tourists, but these and the large number of guest houses, bed and breakfasts and hotels have created a new wealth for the towns where tourism is of major economic importance. The passage of time and introduction of modern life have had little impact on the tranquil yet wild beauty of the region, or its friendly charm and spirit. Cromer and Sheringham are using the strength of their origins to continue building a strong future.

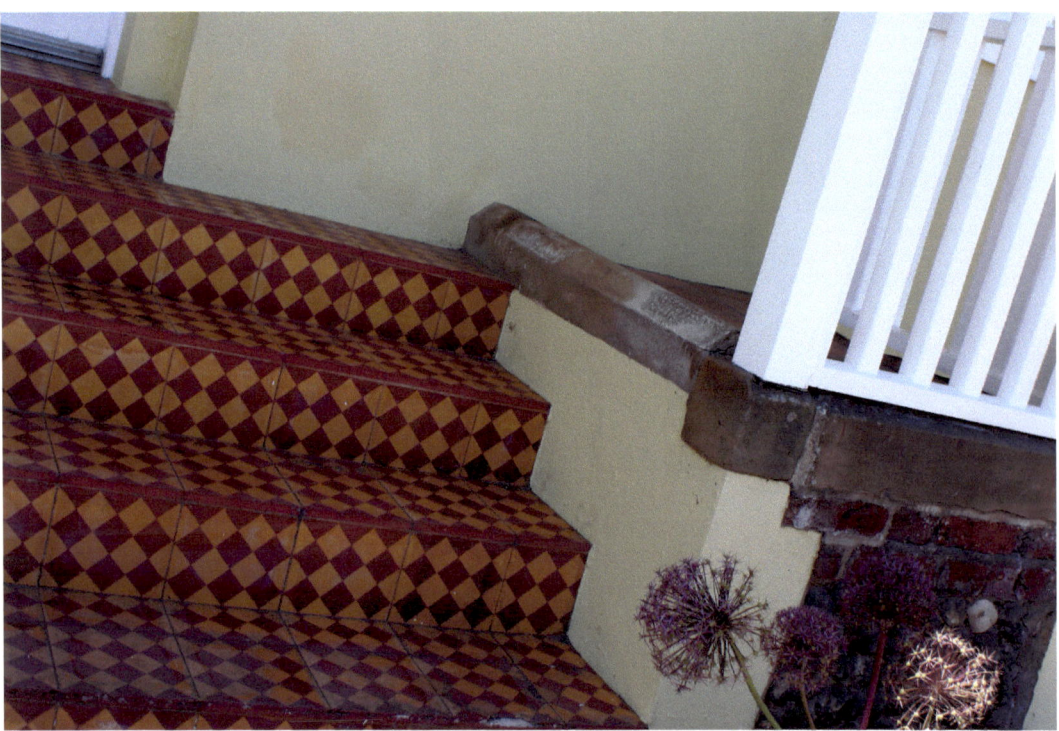

Private homes were altered to become stylish lodging houses.

2. Revealing Churches and Their Tales

The first churches were built in England soon after St Augustine converted Saxon King Aethelbert to Christianity. Since then the church has been both a place of worship and a place of sanctuary. The oldest church buildings around Sheringham and Cromer have not always weathered well, due to both the storms from the sea and the political storms of the sixteenth century when Henry VIII created his own Church of England. During this turbulent period in history a lot of religious imagery and monastic buildings were lost. However, faith remained unconquerable and the church is still the hub of most communities. Many Cromer and Sheringham churches have survived for centuries. Some are new, others have been lost, but none are forgotten. Uncovering the history of the churches reveals both fascinating facts and entertaining stories.

The oldest ecclesiastical building in the Cromer and Sheringham area is the thirteenth-century Augustinian priory at Beeston Regis. It has been abandoned since the Dissolution of the Monasteries and the ruin sits, hidden in trees, next to the original pond that was used by the friars as a source of fresh fish. Most of the domestic buildings that the priory site contained were pulled down to allow the masonry to be reused in the

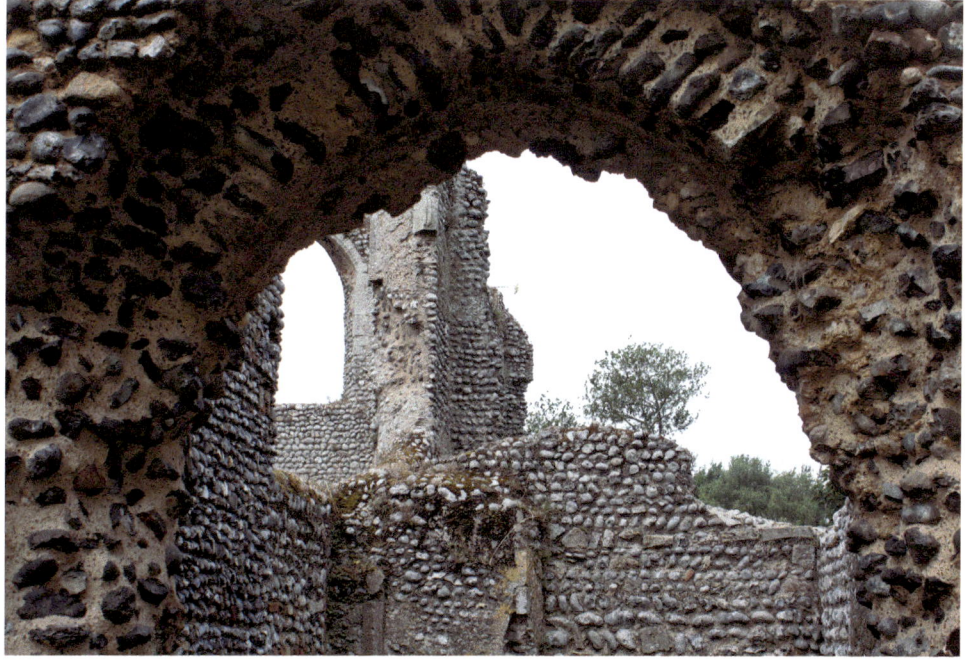

The ruin of Beeston Priory has a hauntingly peaceful setting.

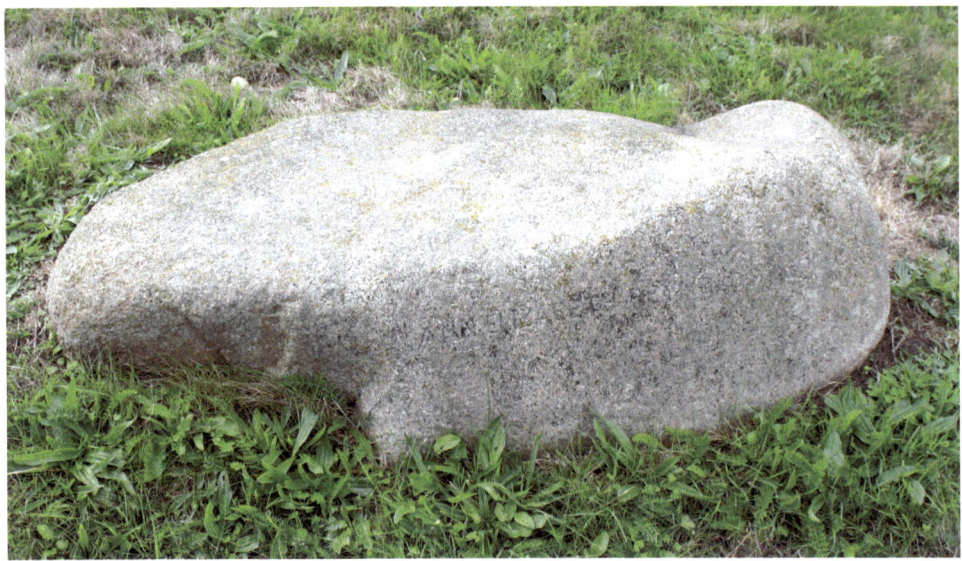

Ghostly occurrences are linked to a block of ecclesiastical masonry.

nearby farms, but the main body of the chapel is still there. The priory is associated with the ghostly tale of 'Farmer Reynold's Stone'. This block of granite used to be on a farm track near the priory ruins. The story goes that when Farmer Reynolds drove his horse and cart into the farmyard at sunset, he often saw a grey, hooded figure hiding behind one particular stone and it would try to grab hold of his horse's reins. The farmer was not unduly worried by the apparition and only said that when he died, he wanted the stone where the phantom had hidden laid onto his grave in the hope that this would lay the troubled spirit to rest. The stone, thought to be part of the chapel stonework, now rests on the grave of James Reynolds. Apparently, the ghost has not been seen since the stone was moved.

All Saints Church in Upper Sheringham and the parish Church of St Peter and St Paul in Cromer date from the fourteenth century but other medieval churches have been lost to the ever-encroaching sea. The village of Shipden Juxta Mare is now all under the sea but it used to be possible to see the remains of the church tower at low tide beyond Cromer pier. It was called Church Rock but was destroyed in the late nineteenth century in a shipping accident.

DID YOU KNOW?
Many churches are dedicated to either St Peter or St Andrew around the coasts. This is also the case in Cromer and Sheringham. St Andrew and St Peter are the patron saints of fishermen and the community in the area wanted blessings from the saints before their families went out to sea to fish.

The medieval church at Sidestrand, just beyond Cromer, teetered on the cliff edge in a ruinous state for many years. Eventually it was decided by the parish to demolish it and use the building materials to rebuild the church. The church was moved stone by stone and St Michael's now stands safely inland. Only the tower of the old church remained near the sea. Writer Clement Scott saw the tower, and the graveyard that still existed around it, and was so moved at its loneliness on the cliff edge that he used the vision for his poem 'The Garden of Sleep'. The writings of Scott took his love of the area, which he dubbed 'Poppyland', to a mass audience and attracted many more tourists. Although attempts were made to keep the old church tower in good repair, it lost its battle with the sea in 1916 and finally toppled from the cliff.

In Sheringham, the Methodist Church of St Andrew, dating from 1968, has strong symbolism relating to the sea. The church tower contains illuminated crosses in the top section that, when lit, can be seen by anyone out at sea. Inside the church the modern stained glass casts a sea-like glow over the pulpit, which is shaped like the prow of a ship. The alms dish, used for congregational collections, is in the form of a shell and the wall behind the pulpit is studded with pebbles from the local beaches. Even the carpet represents the sea and the beach. It is blue in the nave of the church and sandy gold at the east end. Even the word nave has a connection to the sea. It has the same Latin origin as naval, meaning ship, and the ship was an early Christian symbol.

The only building in Sheringham that has Grade II listed status is the Church of St Joseph. This Catholic Church has many fine pieces of early twentieth-century religious art. Opened and dedicated in 1909, it was designed by architect Giles Gilbert Scott. Based

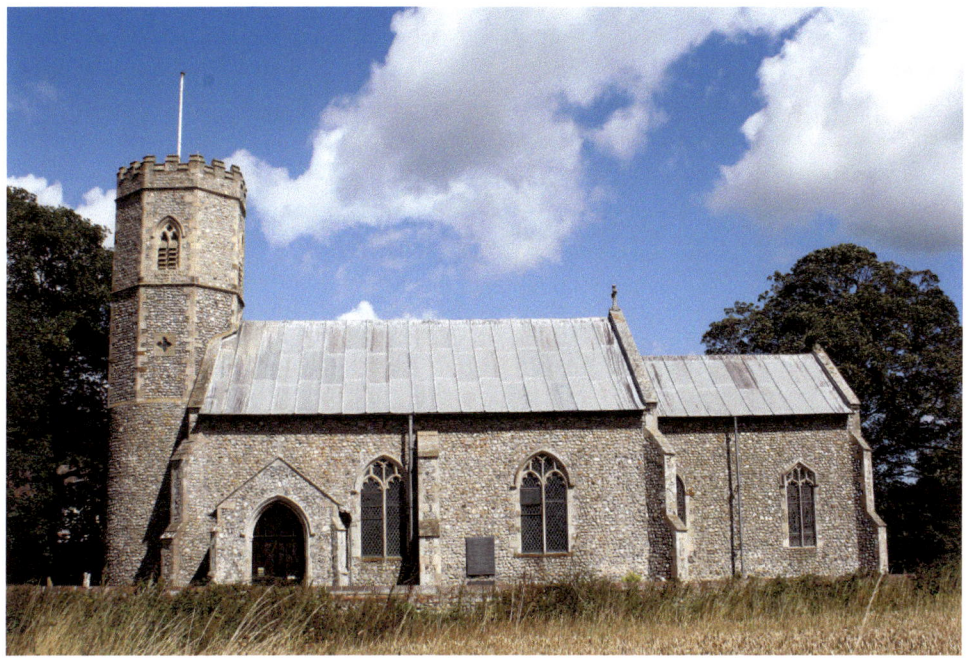

St Michael's, Sidestrand, was rebuilt away from the cliff edge.

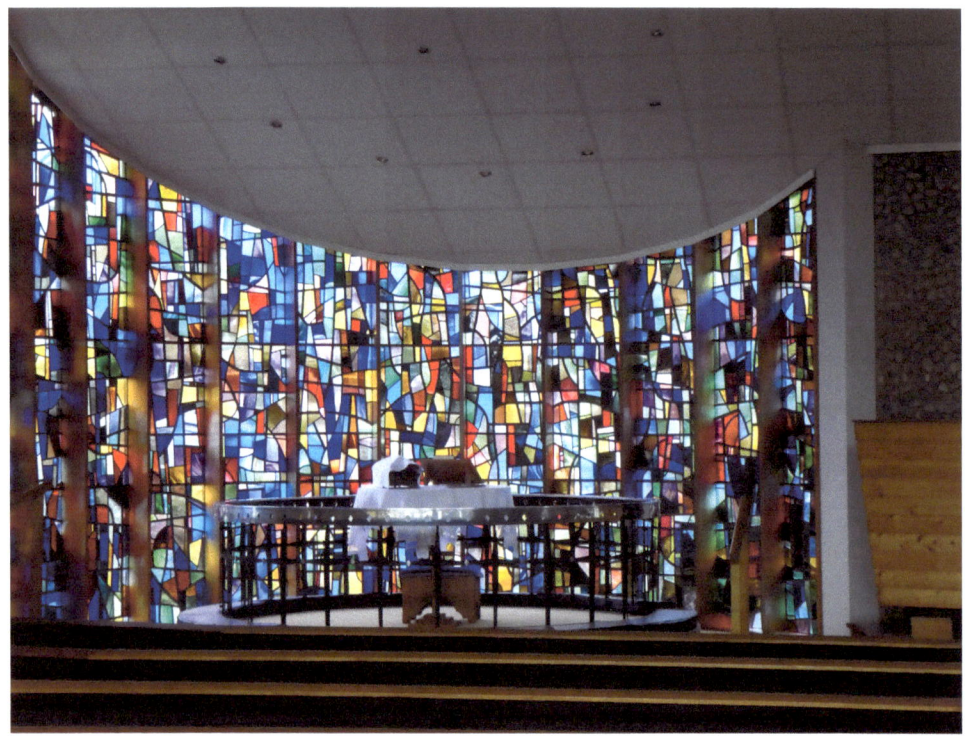

St Andrew's, Sheringham, is filled with modern religious symbolism.

in London, apart from being a prolific ecclesiastical architect, Scott also designed both Battersea Power Station and Bankside Power Station, which later became Tate Modern. The overwhelming size and space of these industrial buildings reflect the light and space that Scott used in his church designs, and the tall red-brick walls of St Joseph's give the church an industrial quality.

The Church of St Peter and St Paul in Cromer is a landmark. It is famed for its 172 steps to the top of the tower and the spectacular views from up there. The church was built in 1377, and before the first lighthouse was built in 1670, beacons were lit at the top of the tower to warn mariners and fishermen of their close proximity to land. Ninety steps up into the tower is a doorway that tradition has called 'Harry Yaxley's Hole'. This doorway accessed a parapet that was used to display lanterns for the benefits of shipping, but it is also known for a curious tale attached to it. It is said that a local lad, Harry Yaxley, with a school friend, rather mischievously used this doorway when no clergy were present to rob a bird's nest on the tower. The nest was a little way below the doorway so Harry was suspended by his feet in an attempt to reach it while the other boy firmly held him by his ankles. The school friend, while holding Harry in this position, decided to try to strike a deal for the major share of any eggs or young birds that Harry stole from the nest. When Harry would not agree to the suggestion, his companion threatened to let go of his ankles. Obviously feeling brave, Harry said, 'Go on then, drop me, because I'm not going to give in to you.' Unfortunately, this is just what happened! Harry fell over 70 feet but, amazingly,

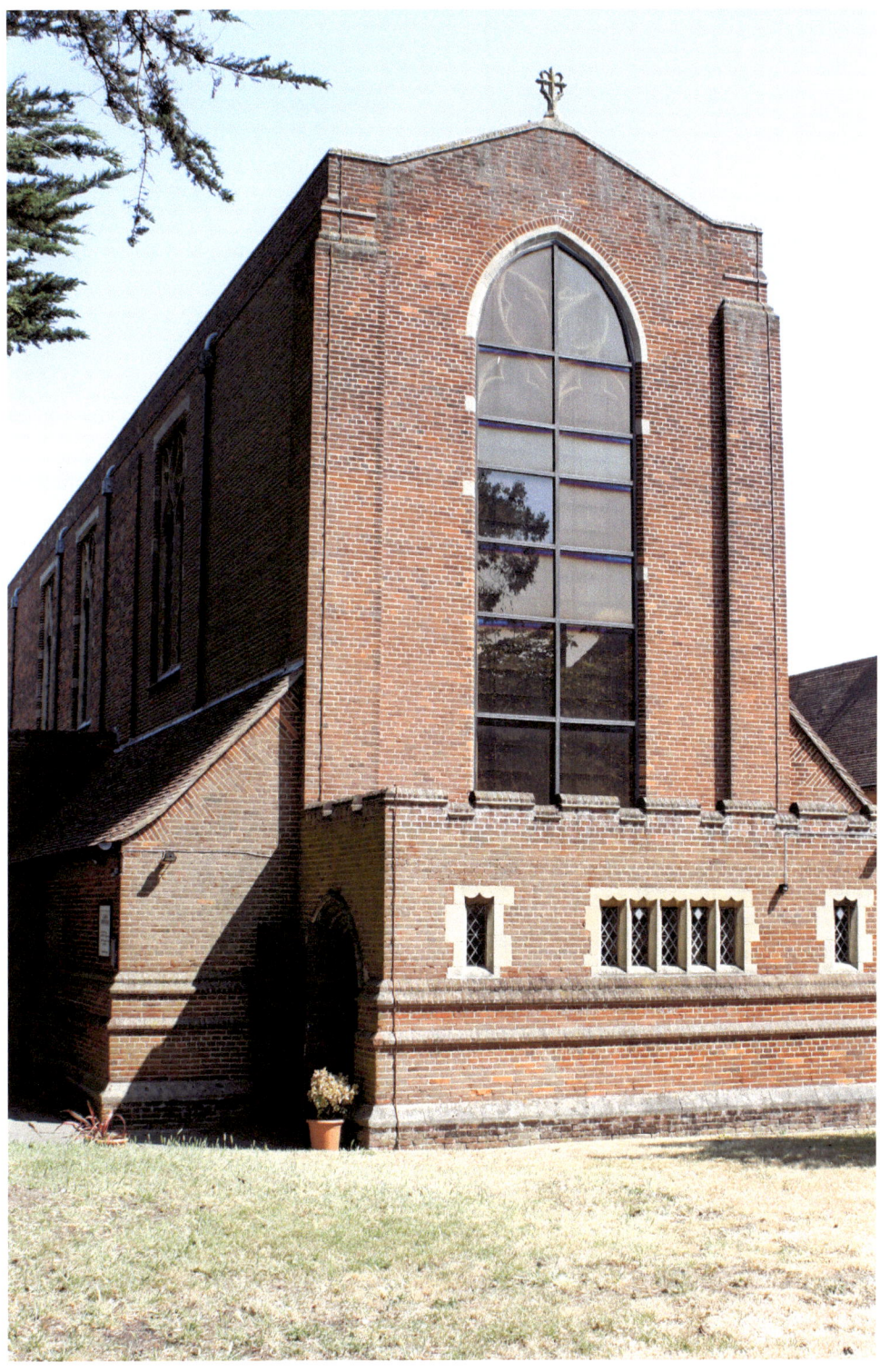

The architect of St Joseph's also designed London's Tate Modern.

landed unharmed. It is unlikely that his companion was as lucky when Harry's father and the local magistrate caught up with him.

Other features of St Peter and St Paul's include a window designed by a famous member of the Pre-Raphaelite movement, Edward Burne-Jones, and another depicting Christ's ascension to heaven that replaces the one destroyed in the 1942 bombing of Cromer. The church has not always been in such a good state of repair as it is now. Before it was completely restored by the Victorians, the church had struggled for years to raise enough money for general maintenance. In 1767 the church had to sell four of its six bells and some of the lead roofing to pay for essential interior repairs. One of the bell ringers was unhappy about losing the bells and remarked that, 'When we consider who this church is dedicated to, it really DOES seem that we are robbing Peter to pay Paul!'

The fourteenth-century All Saints Church in Sheringham has well-preserved medieval woodwork in its rood screen, ceiling bosses and carved pew ends. The symbol of the green man is on the ceiling bosses and is often thought to be a pagan symbol' however, the branches and leaves growing from the face represent growth, new life and resurrection to the Christian faith. The carved ends of the pews in the church include flowers, animals and a swaddled child, but the most famous is that of a mermaid. Legend has it that the mermaid heard hymn singing from the church and came overland from the sea to find out where the wonderful sound was coming from. She knocked on the door of the church and when the very shocked vicar looked down and saw her, he thought she was some form of demon and cried, 'You have no place in this church!' The mermaid crawled away but fearing that she could not make the long journey back to the sea, she rested nearby. When the singing resumed, the mermaid was again entranced by it and moved towards

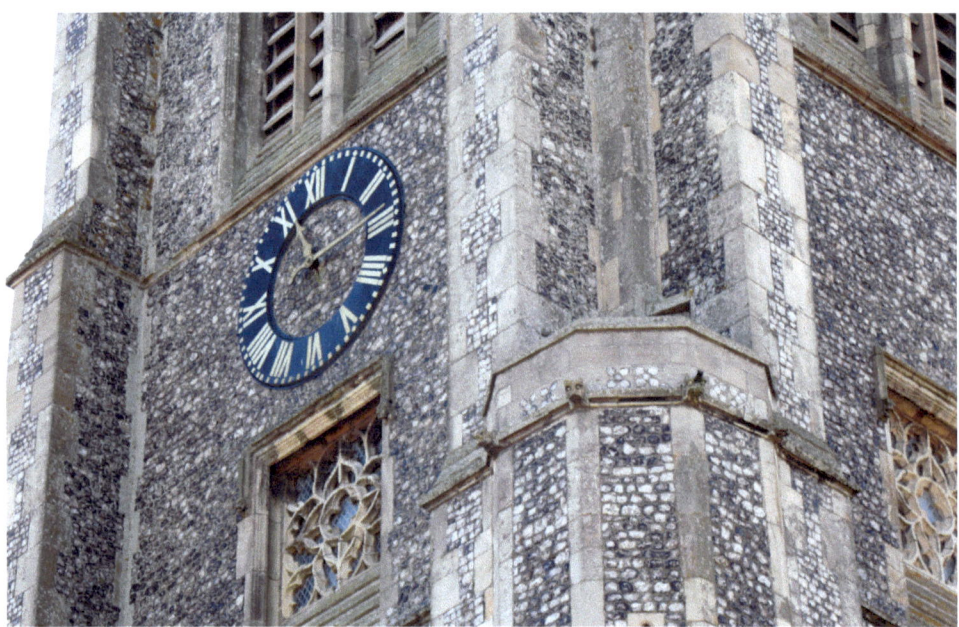

This parapet, 70 feet up Cromer church tower, is legendary.

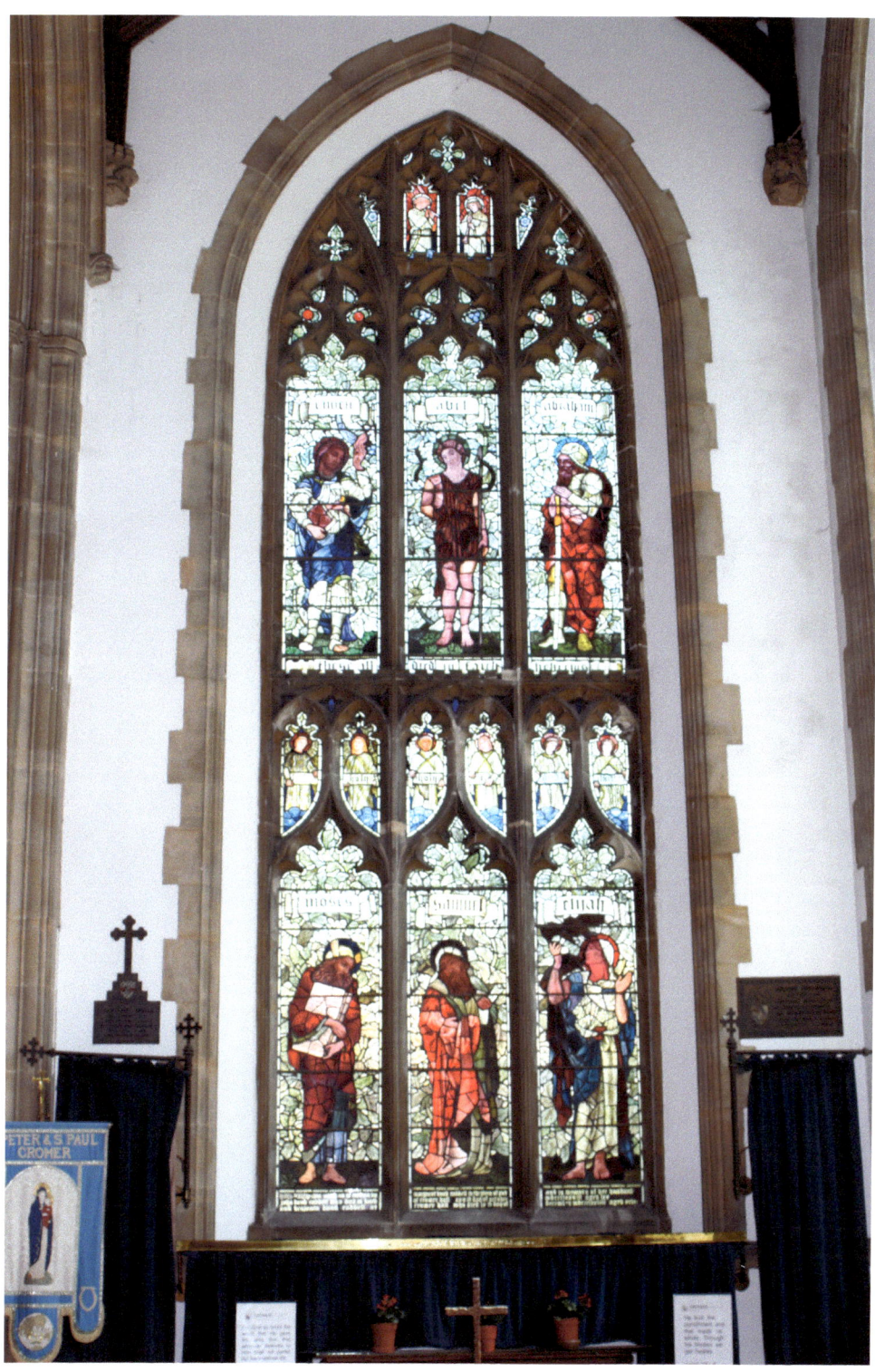

Edward Burne-Jones designed beautiful stained glass for Cromer church.

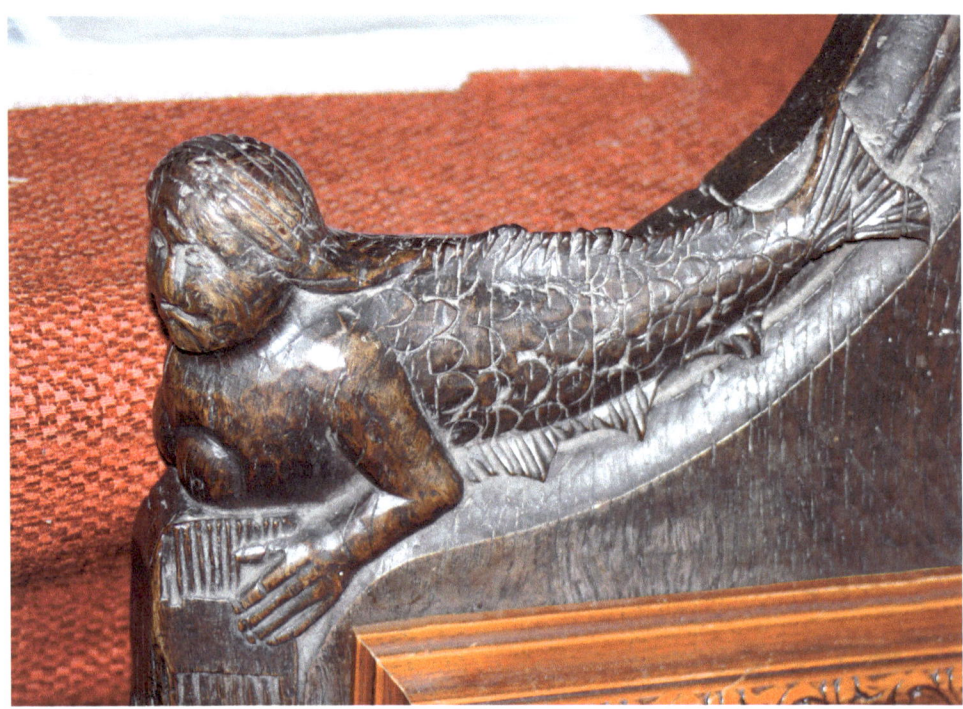

A medieval mermaid still listens quietly in All Saints Church.

the church. The vicar had left the door ajar and she crept inside, taking the rear pew unnoticed. While there, she was so moved by the singing that she vowed to stay to listen more. She did, and the mermaid is still there, on the same pew by the door, listening enraptured to the hymns.

Churches always have hidden stories to tell whether in their architecture, stained glass, woodwork or monuments. Many also have tales of folklore to discover and this is definitely the case for Cromer and Sheringham churches, which are rich in interesting finds.

DID YOU KNOW?
Giles Gilbert Scott was the architect of the Church of St Joseph in Sheringham. He is also famous for being the designer of an essential part of life in the pre-technology era: the telephone box. The first of the Post Office's telephone boxes were introduced in 1920. Considered unattractive, the local councils resisted buying them. Therefore, in 1924, the Post Office ran a competition to design a better one. Scott won and the design was used from 1926. Scott's design showed the boxes painted silver, but the Post Office, to make them more noticeable, chose instead their iconic red.

3. Digging Up Work and Industry

In north Norfolk coastal areas, the environment has created a trade for its population. The sea produced a living for fishermen, the land produced wealth for farmers and the chalky cliffs gave rise to a brick-making industry that made homes for those in the local community. The surrounding land, resources and environment created this economy and, unlike some more industrial areas, the impact on the picturesque landscape has fortunately been slight. It is the unspoilt surroundings near Cromer and Sheringham that now form a vital part of the area's main source of income: tourism.

It can be hard to imagine how a population thrived thousands of years ago but the secret to the progress of Cromer and Sheringham lies in their proximity to the sea. Fishing settlements in the area have existed from prehistoric times due to the relatively abundant food supply from the sea. Archaeologists have found fishing hooks from the Stone Age, and spear fishing was also a common method of hunting. The beaches around Sheringham and Cromer are littered with flint rocks and this made a convenient supply of material for the prehistoric inhabitants to use for tools. They would split the flint nodules and fashion them into spearheads to be used for hunting fish from the shore. Using flint tools and local timber, early man could also make small, basic boats to enable fishing out at sea.

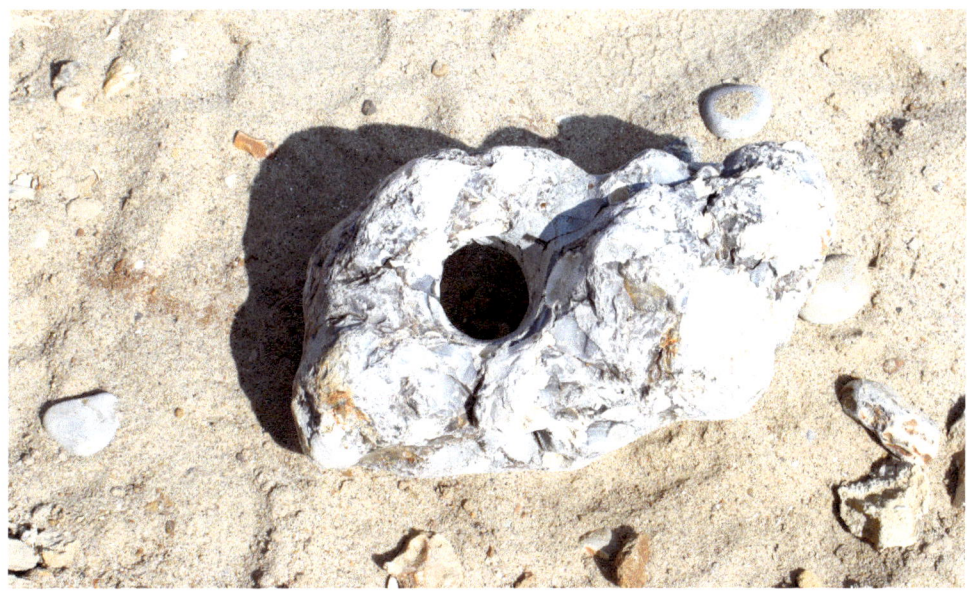

Flint nodules have been used for grinding since ancient times.

These fishing communities gradually grew into villages, and as fishing methods improved and produced a surplus of fish, it meant that the fishermen could trade their catch for other goods and wealth grew.

In the fourteenth century, when the Hundred Years War was ongoing, the fishing trade increased in importance. Fighting men needed food and fish was readily available. Fishing boats worked out of both Sheringham and Cromer to land cod to salt and sell on for vital food supplies for the nation's military. There was no formal navy at this time and private trading boats were often conscripted into service. The king ruled that the fishing fleet of Cromer and Sheringham be exempt from being called on to fight for the Crown as the need for fish was greater than the need for military vessels.

DID YOU KNOW?
All of the slipways down to the beach in the vicinity of Cromer and Sheringham are called Gap. The only access to the sea in this area, with its sheer and fragile cliffs, is where there is a break in the cliff. The term for these routes to the sea was known locally, and literally, as 'The Gap'. To denote which slipway was being referred to, the town or village name was added. Hence we have, East Runton Gap, Sheringham Gap or just The Gap, where boats can launch in Cromer.

As the medieval period continued, the fishing economy continued to flourish and local boats traded in the northern Baltic states as well as Iceland and Greenland. Sheringham, which had been smaller than Cromer before the Tudor era, grew rapidly and by 1800 Sheringham had hundreds of fishing boats. One type of boat was an early trawler called a 'Dogger'. The Sheringham fishermen took these boats north of the Wash to work the fishing grounds at Grimsby and Spurn Head as well as the Sheringham waters. The vast number of trawlers that worked in the area gave rise to its name, Dogger Bank, from which the shipping forecast region gets its name.

The Cromer and Sheringham fisherman traditionally wear dark blue pullovers called Ganseys. A corruption of the name Guernsey, the knitting style began in the sixteenth century in the Channel Islands. These hand-knitted garments are very wind and water resistant and each family or village had their own distinct pattern that the women knitted into the garment. The Sheringham fisherman were known for having the finest and most elaborate patterning in the county. In the unfortunate event that a fisherman drowned at sea, his body could be identified by the individualised stitch work on his gansey and returned to his family for burial.

The sea near Sheringham, sadly, started to become overfished during the nineteenth century and as it could not support all its fishing boats, many fishing families relocated to the Grimsby area or further afield. Despite an upturn in trade when whelk fishing boomed late in the nineteenth century, fishing out of Cromer and Sheringham continued to dwindle and all that is now left of the hundreds-strong fishing fleet that the area

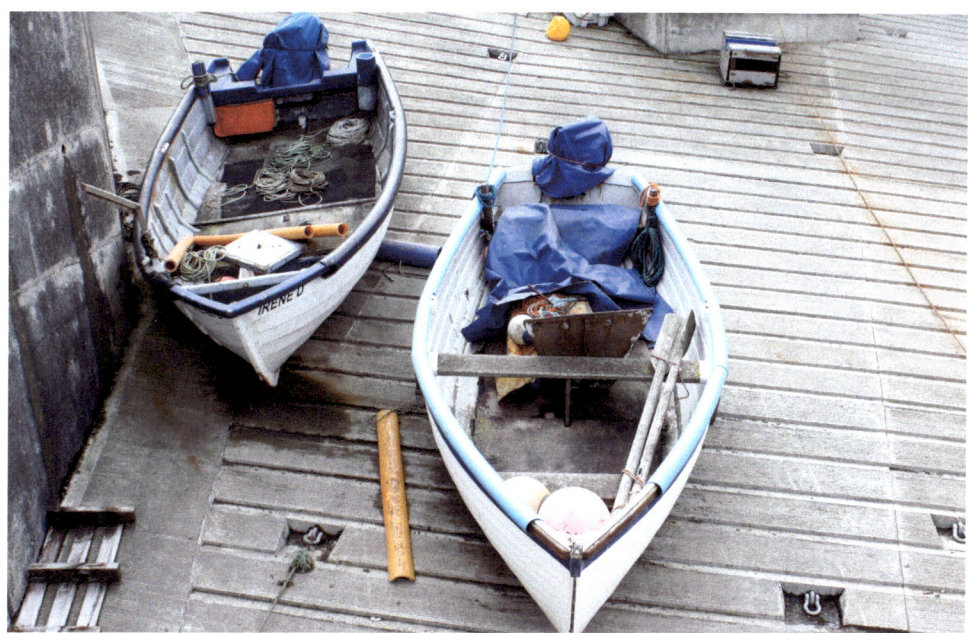

Sheringham fishing boats have changed little in centuries.

once supported are a handful of crab boats. The market for Cromer crab is good and the remaining crab fishermen have a promising economic future.

As the coastline brought prosperity from the sea, so the land also supported its people. The settlement of Upper Sheringham, in the Domesday Book, had livestock listed as '120 pigs, 110 goats, four cows and two horses', which was a lot for a village of its size. In the medieval marketplace these animals would have been an invaluable source of income from dairy products, hides or meat. Not all the land was used to raise animals. There was also a strong arable farming community. Elizabethan documents record that the taxes raised on barley and wheat sales around Cromer and Sheringham were great enough to be used for the upkeep and maintenance of the towns and their slipways, piers and jetties. When, in 1285, Cromer was granted a charter for a weekly market, a wider range of traders came to Sheringham and Cromer, initially for the markets, but they often settled in the towns as a result. They brought with them occupations that the area had not seen before and the community became more diverse as a result.

Flint was another rich resource in the area that created a means of survival. Stone Age man discovered that if flint wasn't readily available on the beach or above ground, it could be mined out of the earth. A flint mine dating from Neolithic times, called Grimes Graves, is a short journey from the Cromer and Sheringham area. The miners used picks shaped from the antlers of red deer to dig deep pits and recover the valuable toolmaking material. When metal eventually replaced flint for toolmaking, the flint miners of the Bronze and Iron Ages used the flints nodules they sourced to build fine houses with. Flint rocks when put together with lime mortar make a valuable building material and can be cut and shaped, or knapped, to make a smooth and attractive wall face.

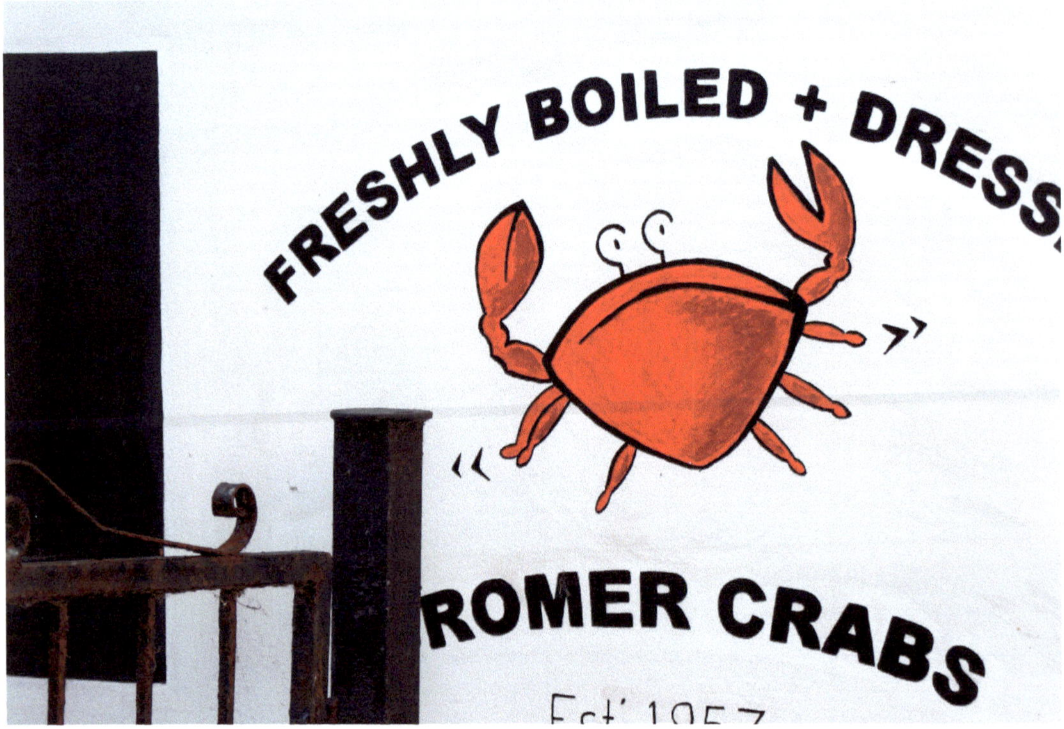

Crabs are both an amusing icon and a lucrative business.

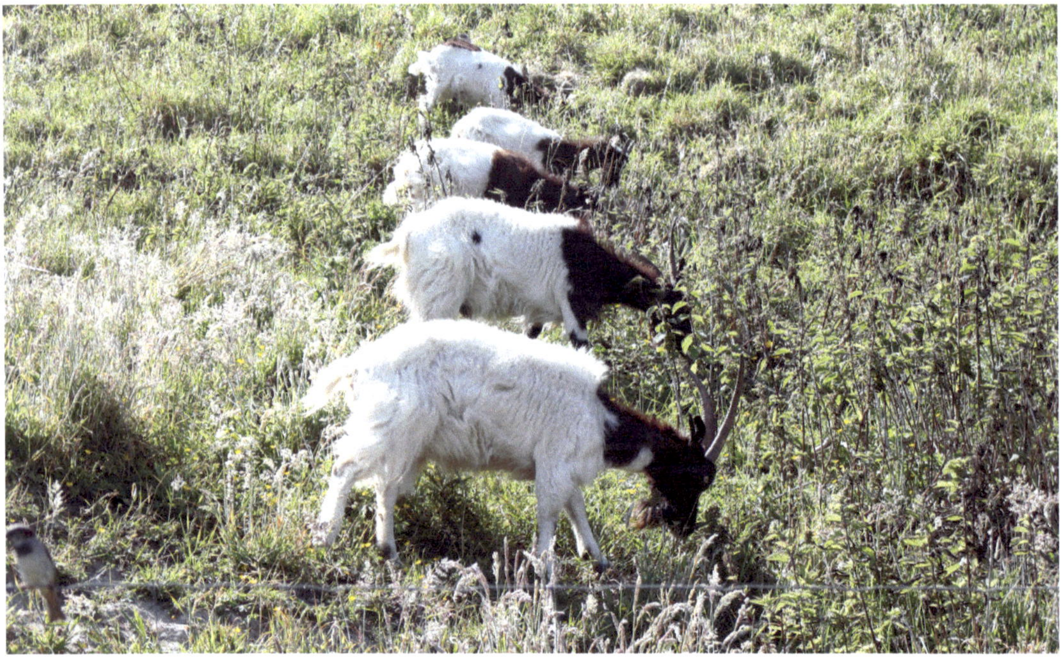

Indigenous goats have grazed around Cromer from the medieval period.

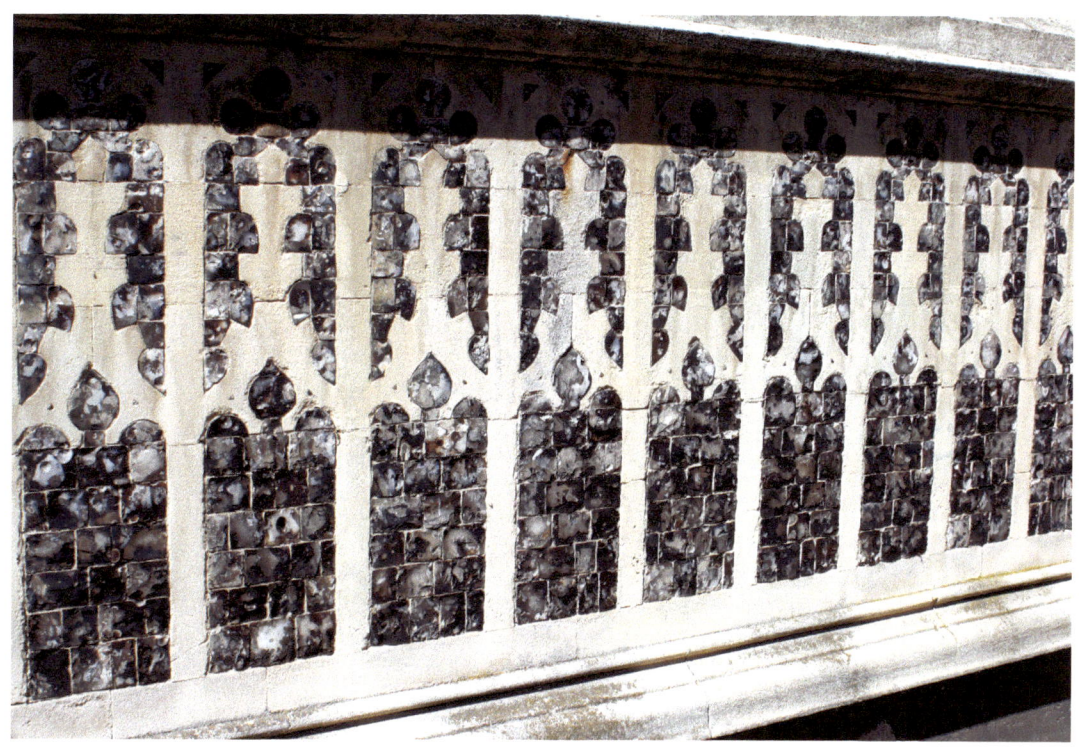

Knapped flint produces an attractive façade for buildings.

The need for houses as the population increased led to the development of the brick industry and brought two new industries to Cromer and Sheringham: brick making and lime burning. Lime is created by burning chalk and has been occurring around Cromer and Sheringham on a small scale for generations. The local area is rich in chalk and the lime it produces when burnt is used to improve the quality of sandy soil, necessary to make good arable land near the coast. Lime is also used in the production of mortar, plaster and limewash, all important elements in house building. As the building trade increased, so the need for lime increased. In the seventeenth century there was a single limekiln in Cromer used for producing lime for soil improvement and small-scale building, but by the nineteenth century many more kilns had been built in the surrounding area. Clay, sand and lime are the components needed for brick making and the abundance of these locally made Cromer and Sheringham prime locations for kilns. The remains of nineteenth-century brick kilns can be seen on the cliffs above Cromer, where an industry built up due to the high demand for property during the Victorian tourist boom.

Not every occupation was entirely legal, and the Cromer and Sheringham area had its fair share of smugglers and pirates. In the fifteenth century, the fishermen of Cromer were granted a licence to carry arms so they could protect themselves from privateers. The permission to travel in armed fleets saved the lives of many Cromer men as the pirates on board these privateers would throw the fishermen overboard after stealing the catch from their boats. The Cromer fishermen were not completely innocent though,

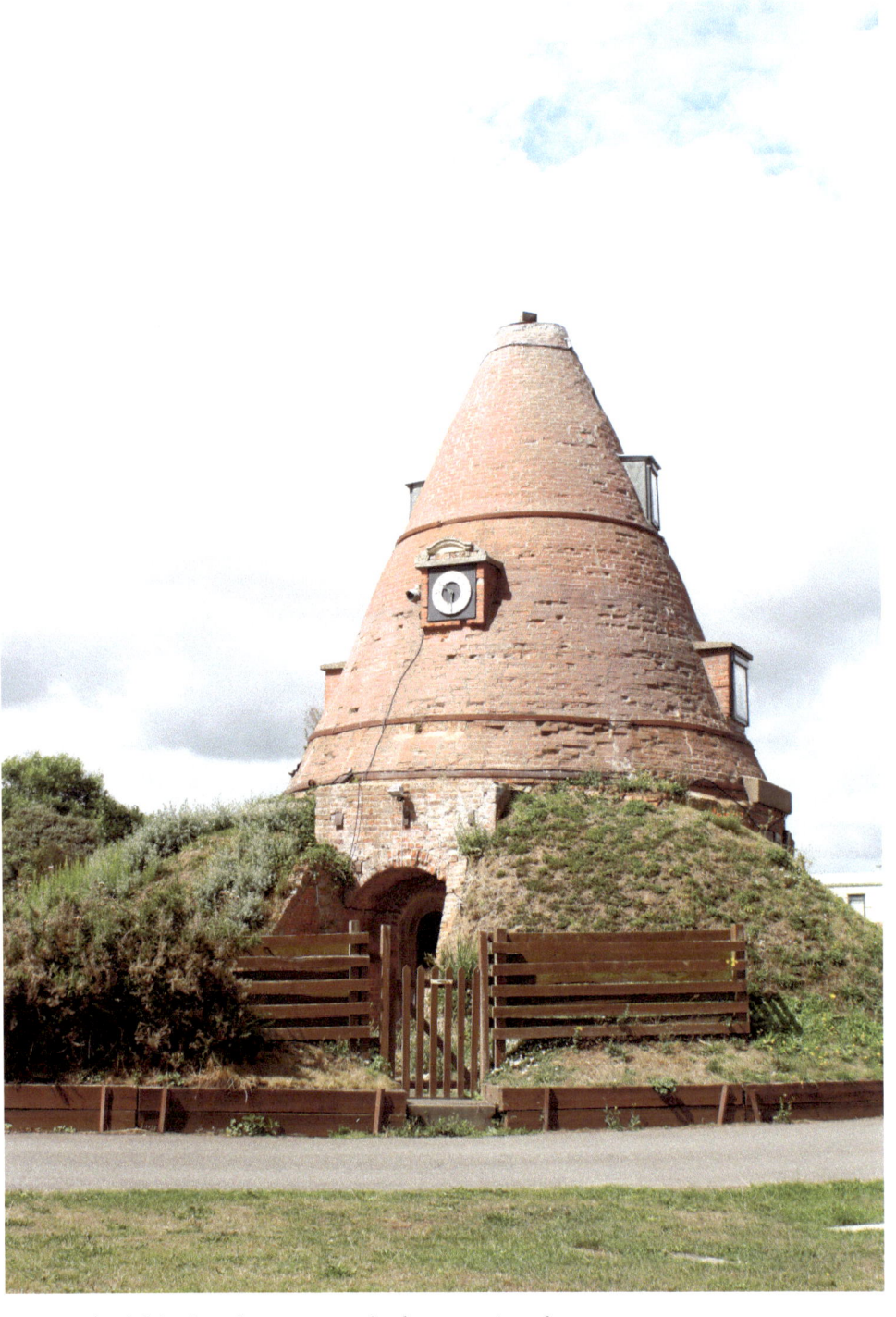

Victorian brick kilns have been renovated to become private homes.

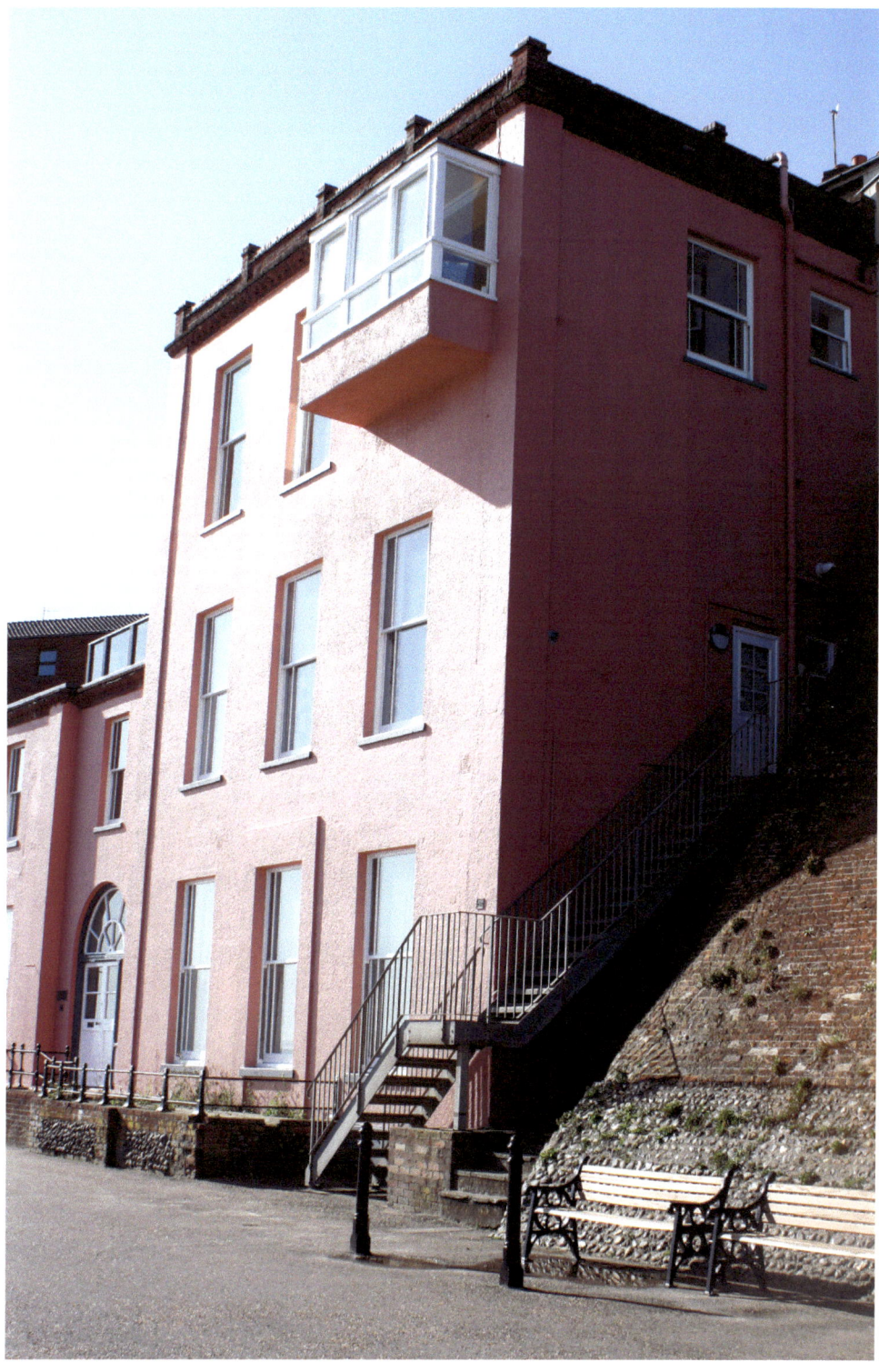

Lookout stations were built to deter and catch smugglers.

and were reported to have been among those responsible for seizing two Dutch ships and bringing them back to shore to sell. The thirty-six sailors and merchants, whose goods they had plundered, were thrown over the side to drown.

Ships landed in Cromer to smuggle goods from early times. Smuggling was often a blatant act as there was only one customs officer to cover the whole of Norfolk, and little chance that he would be in the right place at the right time to confront any smugglers. In the eighteenth century, boats would regularly sail to France to obtain wine, brandy and cloth and bring the goods back to Cromer and Sheringham without paying duty. Smuggling became such a problem that, in 1809, HM Customs and Excise set up stations at regular intervals along the coast to keep a lookout for smugglers' boats and intercept them. The local men could still smuggle goods back to Cromer and Sheringham unnoticed, however, as they knew where the coastal inlets were and could avoid being detected. Smuggling only started to decline as improvements in industry made goods produced in Britain were readily available.

DID YOU KNOW?
In Sheringham the sons of fishermen were usually named after their father. This meant that a lot of families had male members with the same name, including one family who had fourteen Henrys. To distinguish between them, most men were known by a nickname instead. As well as more usual nicknames like 'Young John' or 'Big John', men were known as 'Smiler', 'Windy', 'Big Nose' and 'Crabs', to name but a few. This tradition is still going on today.

The railway came to Cromer in 1877 and to Sheringham ten years later. It created work for the men of the area at a time when the fishing industry was in decline. After its completion, the railway brought with it the industry that is now the largest in the Cromer and Sheringham area: tourism. The railway made travel easier and more affordable, and Clement Scott had popularised the Cromer and Sheringham area with his 'Poppy land' writings, which attracted the middle classes to the resorts. The visitors needed accommodation, refreshment and entertainment and many new hotels and boarding houses were built. Private homes were converted into guest houses and eating and drinking establishments opened, all creating work for residents. The local people turned to offering goods and services to tourists as means to make a living and providing for visitors has been the major source of income for the last 150 years.

How a town generates its livelihood is not always obvious. It is no longer working the land or fishing the sea that brings prosperity to Cromer and Sheringham. It is catering for the needs of the visitors who come to enjoy the area. The land and sea that tourists now come to enjoy the view of is the same land and sea that generations of local people had worked so tirelessly on as a means to provide for themselves and their families. Now, most of these families get their income from the tourists.

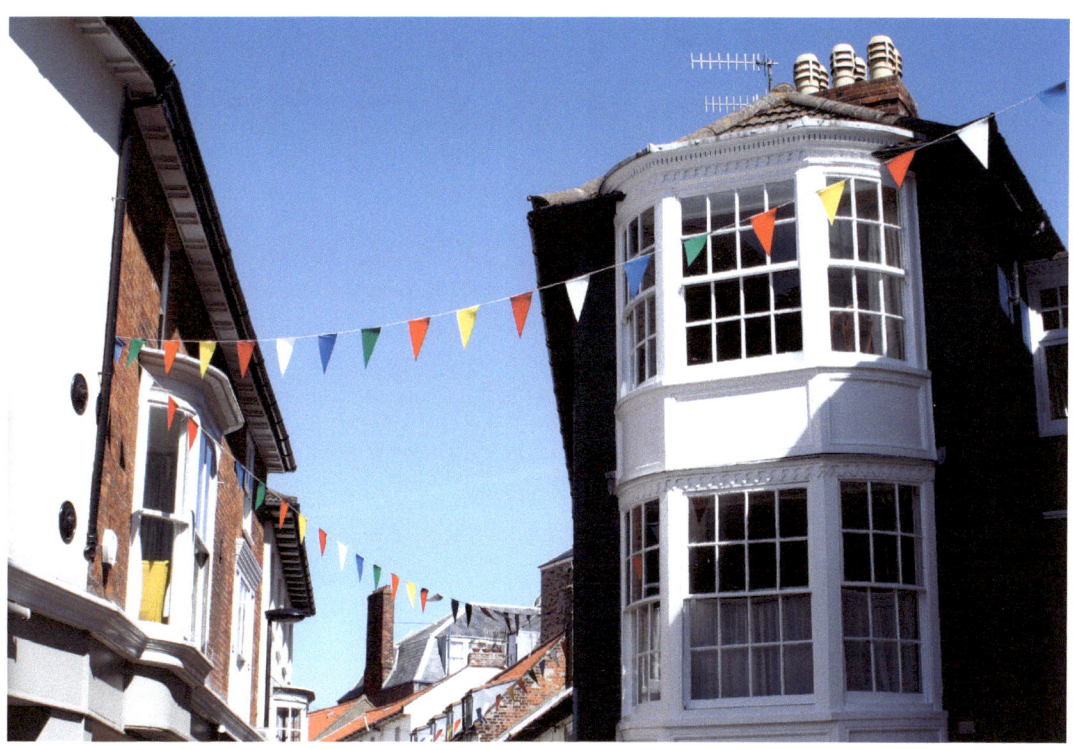

Medieval street layouts now have more modern properties on them.

DID YOU KNOW?
In the Domesday Book, the original settlements of Cromer and Sheringham were each listed as having fifty to sixty goats. Sheep have replaced the goat as farm livestock but Cromer still has a use for goats. A surprising sight to visitors is the herd grazing on the fenced-off incline from the sea wall up to the Promenade. They are Bagot goats. The ancient breed has been put there by the local council as a very 'green' way to keep litter and vegetation down on the steep bank. They have become much loved by Cromer residents.

4. The Hidden Past of Tourism

Tourism and enjoying time at leisure is often thought to be a creation of modern society but this can be revealed as untrue. Even prehistoric man employed a kind of tourism. The game that he hunted moved location according to season, migrating to where food sources were plentiful. When the animals moved to warmer climates in the cold weather, primitive man followed to seek the sun.

By the time of the Roman Empire, a more recognisable form of holidaying existed. Due to the excellent road system that the Romans had created and kept maintained, the rich Anglo-Roman people could take time away from the towns like Leicester or St Albans to enjoy peace and fresh air at coastal locations. There was a definite tourist economy as organisers would arrange transport, accommodation and entertainment for the travellers. When the Roman Empire collapsed so did the road system, and the ability to travel easily and safely became impossible.

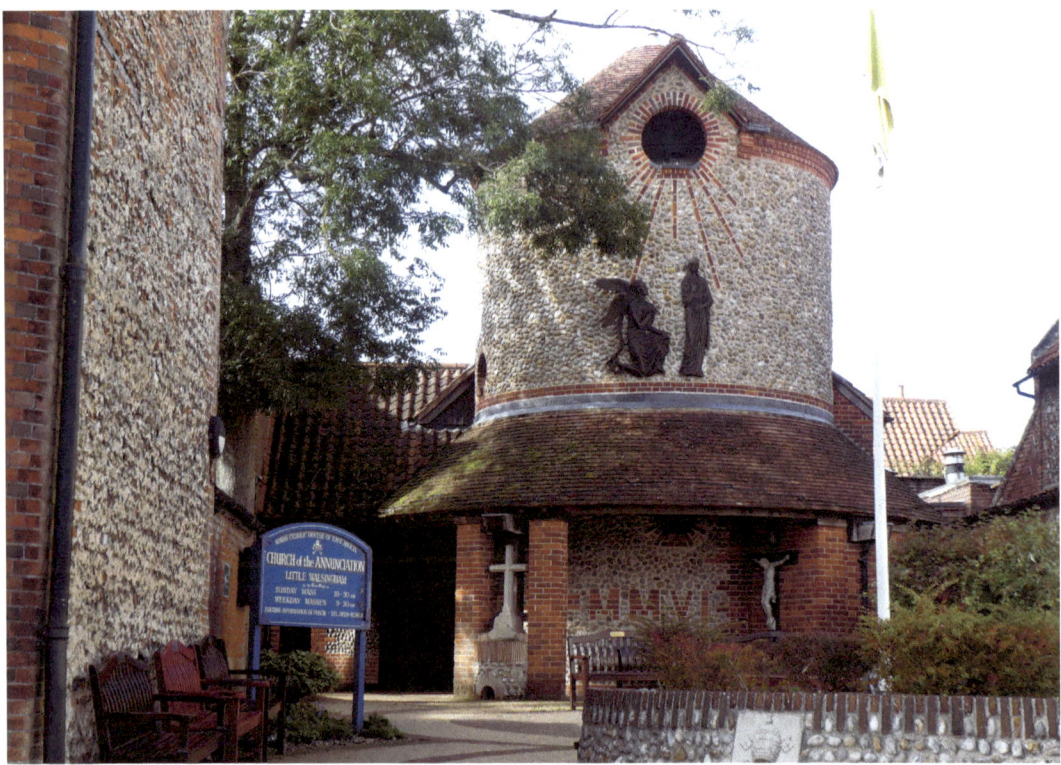

Pilgrims have visited Little Walsingham for half a millennium.

It wasn't until medieval times that the idea of taking holidays re-emerged. There were many religious shrines around the country and the pious or rich would take pilgrimages of many miles to visit a holy site and receive blessings. There is a shrine near Cromer and Sheringham at Little Walsingham that has been a visitor attraction for over 500 years. The word holiday dates from the fourteenth century when *The Canterbury Tales* was written by Geoffrey Chaucer about a group of travellers on a pilgrimage. The pilgrimage was for a 'holy day' or 'holiday', as it became corrupted to.

It was when 'taking the waters' became a fashionable health pursuit in the late eighteenth century that the rich began to take holidays in earnest. Inland spa towns, situated near thermal springs, started to attract wealthy visitors but so did seaside resorts like Sheringham and Cromer, where the seawater and clean air, of which there was a plentiful supply, were a draw to this new type of holidaymaker. Gradually, the desire to take time away from home, even if it was not for health reasons, increased and the classic British seaside holiday began to evolve. The constantly improving rail infrastructure allowed travel to become more affordable and available to all, and by the late nineteenth century the tourist and leisure industry in Cromer and Sheringham was firmly established.

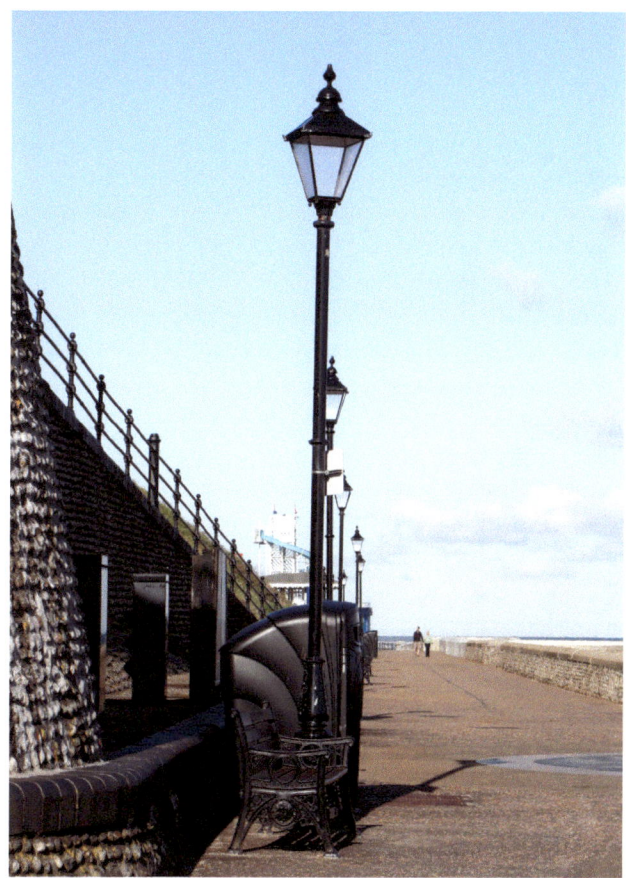

Clean fresh air and a sea view attracted promenading visitors.

In the late eighteenth century neither Cromer nor Sheringham had been equipped for the increase in visitors, and accommodation was in short supply. There were only four hostelries in Cromer and a couple of inns in Sheringham. Many rich banking families from Norwich had taken to holidaying around Sheringham and Cromer and they bought land in the local area on which to build large houses. Visiting friends would stay as guests in these large houses and this accommodated some, but the demand for public lodging was high.

DID YOU KNOW?
When Cromer pier was opened in 1901 there was a strict view regarding the etiquette of those using it. A notice stated, 'On a Sunday, all servants in livery, and common persons, are not allowed' and also, 'The commissioners forbid the smoking of cigars until nine o'clock in the evening when ladies will have retired from the pier.' This concern for female well-being was not apparent, however, when the pier refused to provide toilet facilities for women, stating, 'there is adequate provision in the council conveniences by The Red Lion Steps and they are barely half a mile away'.

One of the first people to try to provide for this need was Pierre Le Francoise. He bought a maritime villa that had been recently constructed for Lord Suffield as a holiday home. He altered it, extending the property to become the commanding seafront Hotel de Paris. The Le Francois family had been refugees from the French Revolution and forced to leave France, eventually settling in Cromer. Pierre's family were still proud of their roots as is evident in the name and French styling of the hotel. Entrepreneurs bought more houses to convert into accommodation and hotels and guest houses were newly built all along the promenade.

The French word '*promenade*' has been used in the English language to mean 'go for a gentle walk' for centuries. By the early nineteenth century the meaning had altered to be synonymous with 'a walk by the sea' to such an extent that the path visitors used for their picturesque stroll became known as the Promenade. The sea walls in Cromer were built in 1838 to protect the town from the encroaching sea and were a pleasant place to promenade. Although the walls ended by the pier, there was a further walk up to the lighthouse on the cliffs through an area that became known as Happy Valley where railings and gateposts marking the path the Victorians took can still be seen.

The most iconic sight in Cromer is the pier. The version now standing, though much restored, is late Victorian, and no photograph, painting or drawing of Cromer seems complete without the pier to grace it. Every visitor rushes to visit this epitome of the British seaside. Whatever the weather, even in the depths of winter, there are hardy souls sitting in the shelters and enjoying the sea.

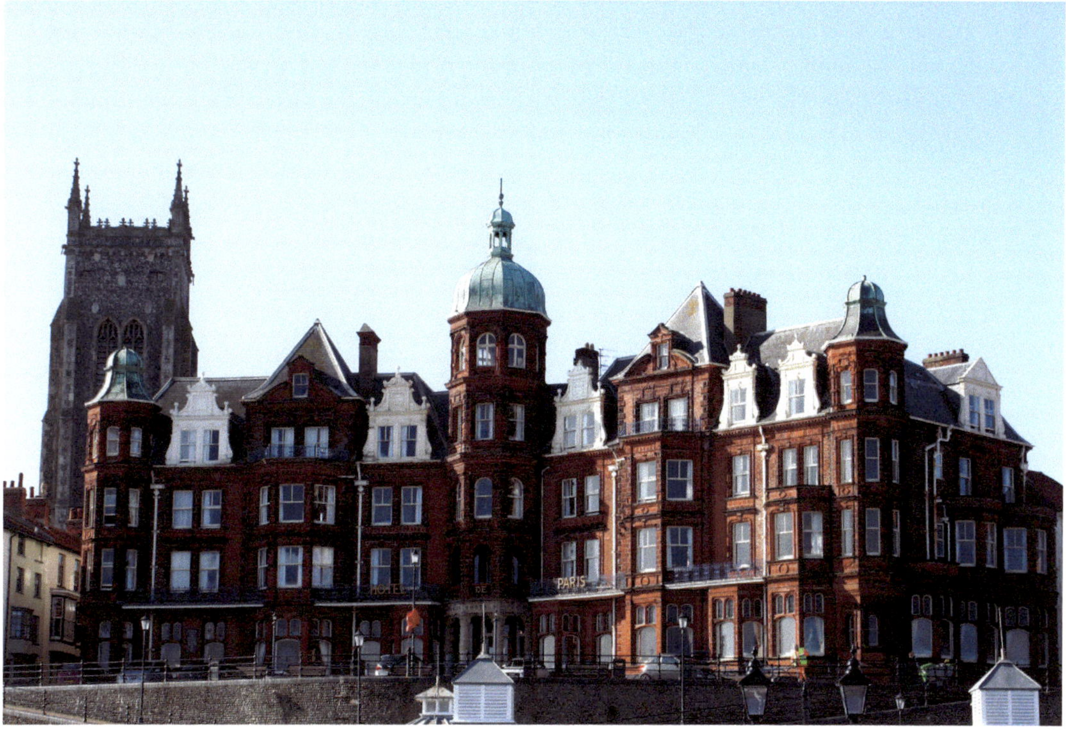

The Hotel de Paris stands in front of Cromer pier.

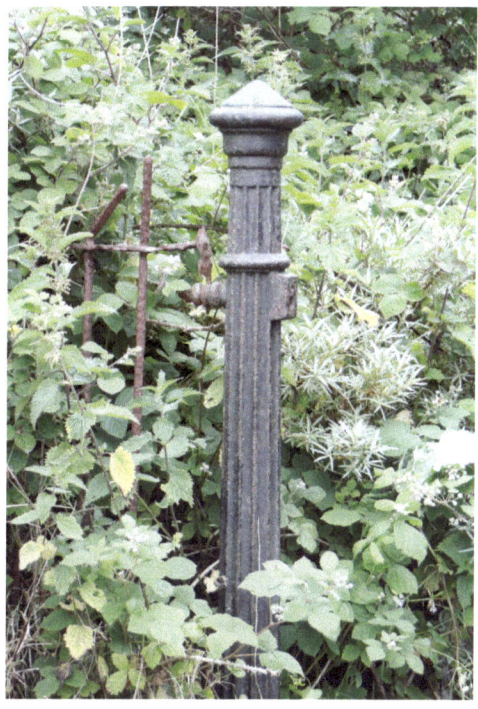

Victorian railings still mark pathways in
Happy Valley.

There has been some form of pier around this site since the first stone jetty was built to enable shipping to land safely well over 600 years ago. In 1390, Richard II granted the people of Cromer the right to use taxation monies to build the desperately needed pier. Navigation in the area around the shore was very poor. Land slips were a problem and properties would fall with the cliffs and be washed out to sea, making piloting around Cromer very hazardous. The first pier was a stone quay and it was a safe landing place for all mariners and fishermen. The power of the sea caused constant damage, however, and although there were appeals to raise money for the pier upkeep there was little success and the stone pier gradually deteriorated.

DID YOU KNOW?
During the 1960s and 1970s, Cromer had a zoo quite unlike the one it has now. It was a rather shabby tourist attraction opened by circus performer Olga Kerr. She was the daughter of the most famous circus clown at the time, Coco the Clown. A main attraction was Billy the chimp, who apparently smoked a pipe and any cigarettes he could beg from visitors. After her husband died, Olga couldn't support the zoo and it closed in 1983. All the animals were rehomed except the last lioness. She managed to escape and unfortunately had to be shot.

Funds from the Crown meant the pier could be completely rebuilt during the Elizabethan era. The Elizabethan pier was a simple wooden jetty and did not fare well with the bad weather. In 1822 a cast-iron pier was built in the hope it could better withstand the elements. Ironically, after just twenty years, this too was lost in a storm.

The town was becoming popular with tourists and an esplanade where people could stroll was created in 1848. Another wooden pier replaced the cast-iron one and tourists started to enjoy promenading along it as part of their esplanade walk, even though it was still very much a working quayside used by fishing boats. Over the next fifty years the fishing trade dwindled and tourists took over from the fishermen and sailors as the main users of the pier.

The structure was gradually strengthened and improved but it was the Victorian ladies and their fashion consciousness that led to the demise of the final wooden pier. Victorian ladies liked to wear stiletto heels and the women complained that their heels were getting stuck between the slats on the pier. It was decided to replace the open wooden slats with solid planking to prevent damage to the ladies' shoes. This decision directly led to the whole of the decking being ripped off in a storm. Where the wind and high waves had previously been able to pass through the open slats, the solid planking created an impermeable barrier. Storm force winds got under the pier and lifted the deck up and off, taking other pier structures with it. The pier was left in ruins and a completely new structure was needed to replace it.

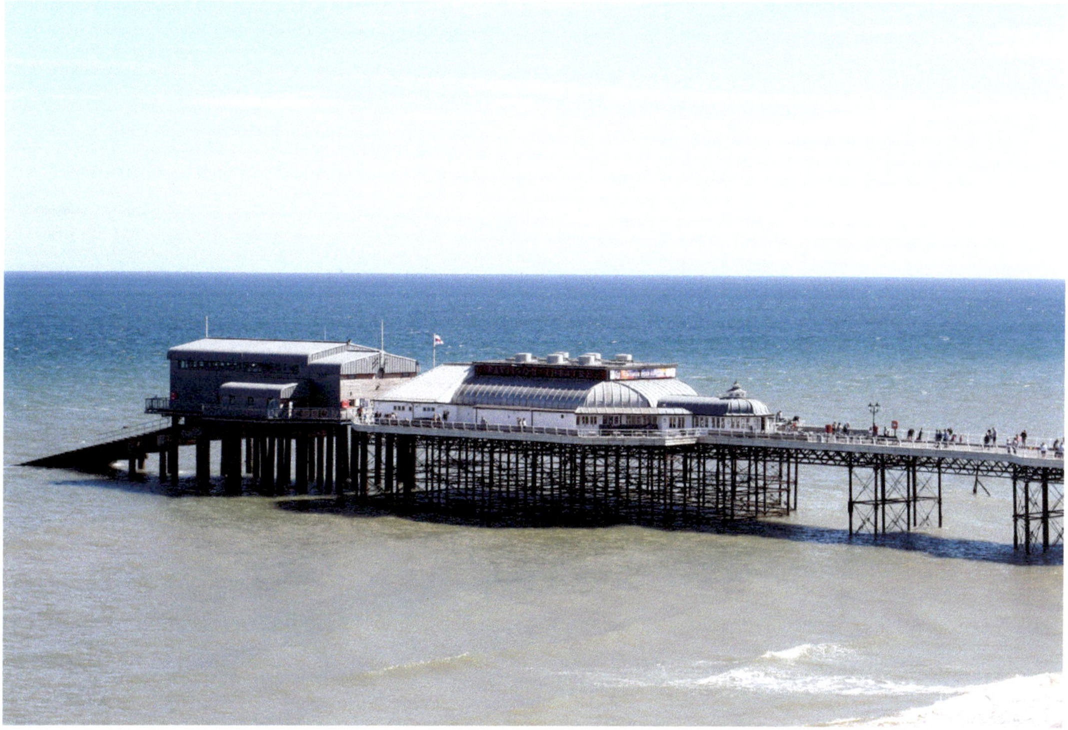

Cromer pier is an iconic view.

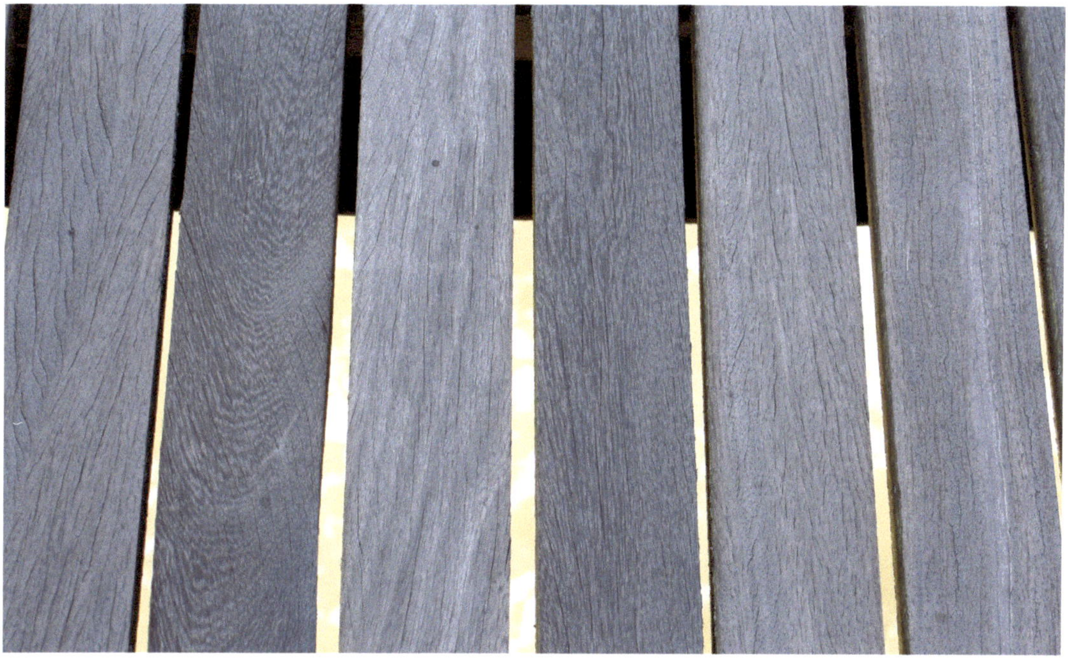

Slatted wooden decking trapped the shoe heels of Victorian ladies.

In 1901, a brand new cast iron pier was opened, and this is the one that stands today. It was built and equipped for the tourists who wanted to use it. There were seated shelters to protect promenaders from the elements and a bandstand to entertain those using it. The pier was now purely for recreation and no boats except the lifeboat ever docked there. By the 1920s the bandstand and shelter at the end of the pier were combined to create a large covered pavilion. A stage was added to create a theatre and facilities for refreshments were added. The Pavilion Theatre has since been used for all sorts of light entertainment including operas, popular bands and variety shows. It is the variety show that now makes Cromer pier unique. During the last decades of the twentieth century, the popularity of the 'Seaside Special' show that had been so favoured twenty years earlier was at an end. While many piers stopped putting on light entertainment in this way, Cromer pier steadfastly refused to cancel their Seaside Special and now it has come through the decades of unpopularity to become in demand again as the only pier in the world with a variety show of this kind. The Cromer End of the Pier Show is a charming and vibrant production and rightly deserves its new-found fame.

However, during the 1950s it was decided that the pier was not enough of an attraction for modern visitors who, according to the town council, 'Didn't want to just walk down to the end and sit there freezing.' In an attempt to make it more viable, two amusement arcades were added. The rather incongruous structures lasted for around thirty years until a fierce storm and 100 mph winds unceremoniously removed them.

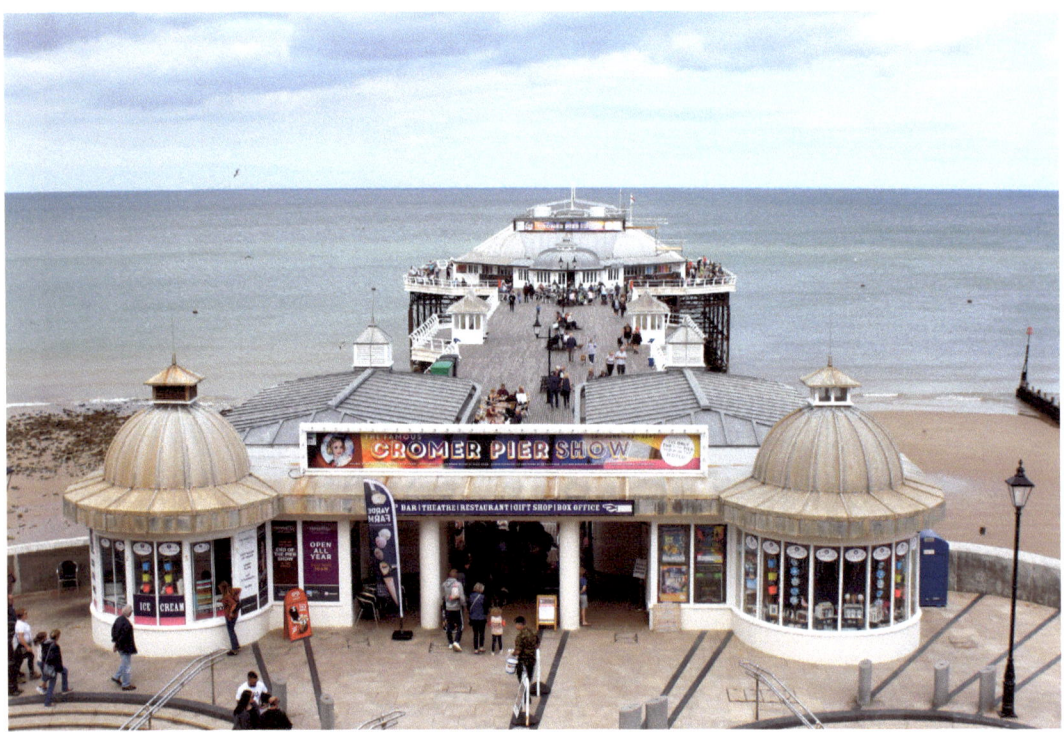

Cromer pier's variety show is the last of its kind.

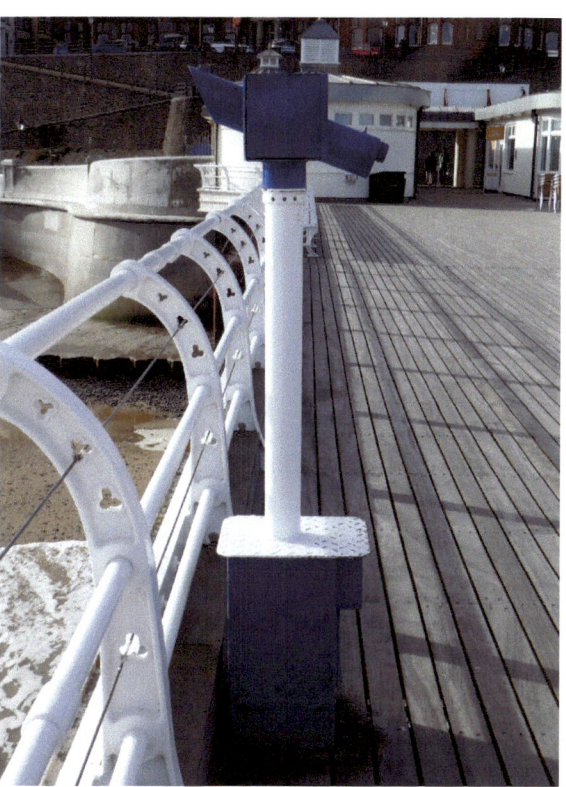

Constant maintenance is needed to
preserve the pier's charm.

Always at the mercy of the weather, the 1953 storm surge caused untold damage to the
pier at a time when it had only recently reopened after the years of the Second World
War. Nearly every following decade saw damage and repair and then in 1993 the pier was
torn in half by a drifting sea platform. The platform, the Tayjack, had been working a mile
out to sea when a storm sheared it from its legs, removed the deck cranes and sent the
main body of the structure hurtling back to shore. It struck the seafront at Cromer taking
out the centre of the pier and many wooden groynes. The pier was now unreachable
from the shore. As it was vital that the lifeboat station could be reached, a simple rope
suspension bridge was strung across the gap in the pier to allow the lifeboatmen access to
their station. This colossal breach caused by the Tayjack was, fortunately, repaired within
just six months.

The constant maintenance of the pier, where perhaps others would have been allowed
to fade away, shows the importance of the pier to Cromer. The pier in the twenty-first
century would never be considered 'not interesting enough', as it was in the 1950s when
the amusement arcades were added. The reason people want to visit the pier is precisely
because it is a place to just sit and watch the sea and the birds, or wander down to watch
the numerous fishermen or children with their crab buckets. The once unpopular End
of the Pier Show is a constant sellout in the summer, with a Christmas show bringing in
winter visitors and, despite the pier having had more damage from the ferocious weather
than most could bear, it is an ever-present, bright, happy tourist haven.

DID YOU KNOW?
The first caravan used for holidaying was made in 1880 for Dr William Stables, a travelling writer who called himself a 'Gentleman Gypsy'. When he came to either Cromer or Sheringham in his basic caravan he found it rather chilly. A Victorian postcard from Cromer said, 'No hope of bathing this holiday, almost ice floating about.' It was posted in June. A guesthouse in the 1920s revealed the effect of the weather: 'Due to rain it has been a bad summer for lettings. I cannot pay my rent this season.' Hopefully, the sun shone the following year for them.

The pier wasn't the only source of entertainment for the tourists to Cromer, the first cinema in the town opened in 1914. This was the Regal and it is still a cinema, although refurbished and a modern multiscreen complex. The Casino cinema, in Sheringham, also opened in 1914 but this has since been converted to become the Masonic Hall. Before the cinemas were built any cinematographic performances were shown in the town halls but when Sheringham's largest cinema, the Picture Palace, opened, it was used for public meetings as well as films due to its large size and replaced the town hall for many events. The Picture Palace went on to be converted into Sheringham's Little Theatre, which continues to attract many visitors to its plays and performances.

Forerunners to the cinemas were the magic lantern displays that delighted audiences with their moving pictures. These were regularly put on to entertain people in both towns. Cromer, for some years from 1880, also boasted a Camera Obscura in a dark tent near the gangway, where amazed Victorians could look down to see a wide view of the town.

Sheringham had an open-air theatre, the Arcade Lawn. Situated in the older part of the fishing town, it was not the most professional venue; the stage was roofed with corrugated iron and the audience had to sit out in all weathers. It was close to many of the fisherman's terraces and the locals used to balance on chairs by the windows of their homes to get a view of the entertainment without having to pay. The children of the town took an alternative pleasure from the Arcade Lawn. Boys and girls would sit on the pavement watching the carriages from the new hotels as they passed by on their way to the evening's performance. They enjoyed gazing at the finery of the rich tourists and their horse-drawn vehicles, and playing make-believe that one day it would be them.

The idea of a fête or carnival goes back to the time when Cromer was granted a charter for a week-long fair back in the medieval period. As well as somewhere to trade, this would have involved some kind of street entertainment. It was early in the nineteenth century, with the burgeoning tourist population, that pleasure fairs began. Cromer and Sheringham now hold carnivals over the summer season that appeal to both tourists and locals alike. From Victorian times the Whitsun Fair in Cromer involved all kinds of popular beachfront entertainment including Punch and Judy and donkey rides for the children. When the new pier opened in 1901, this changed to become the Pier Carnival and was held for a week in August, the height of the tourist season. It included fancy dress parades and competitions, boat races and, in the 1920s, there was a fire diver who

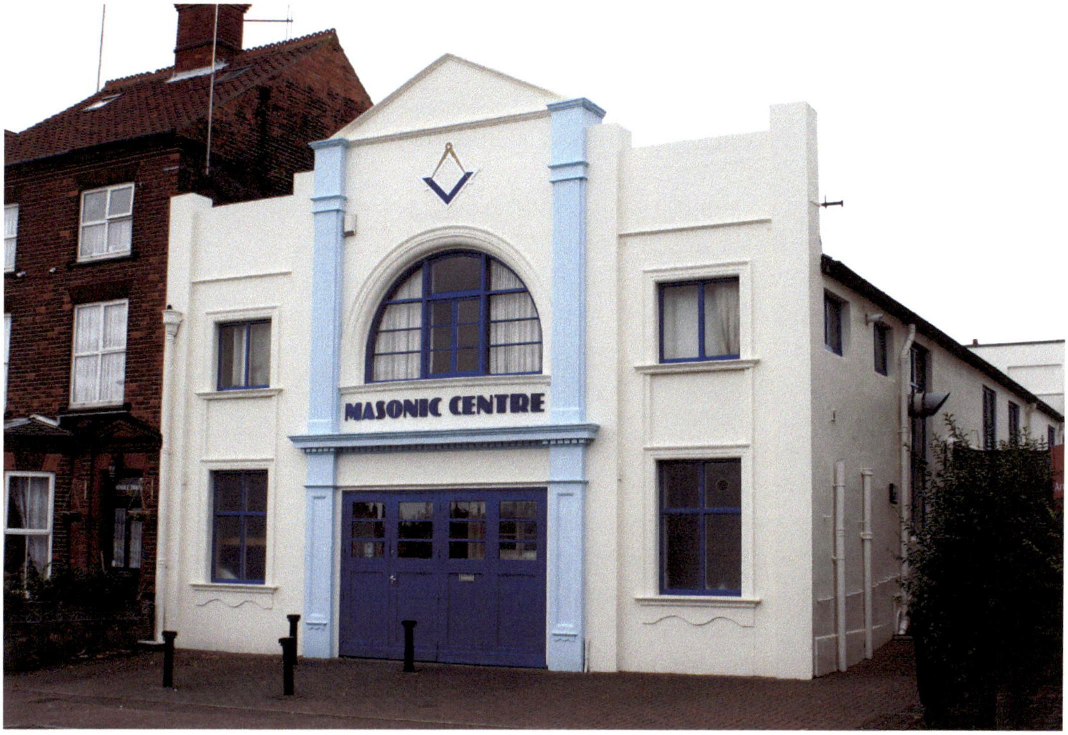

Sheringham's first cinema, the Casino, is now the Masonic Hall.

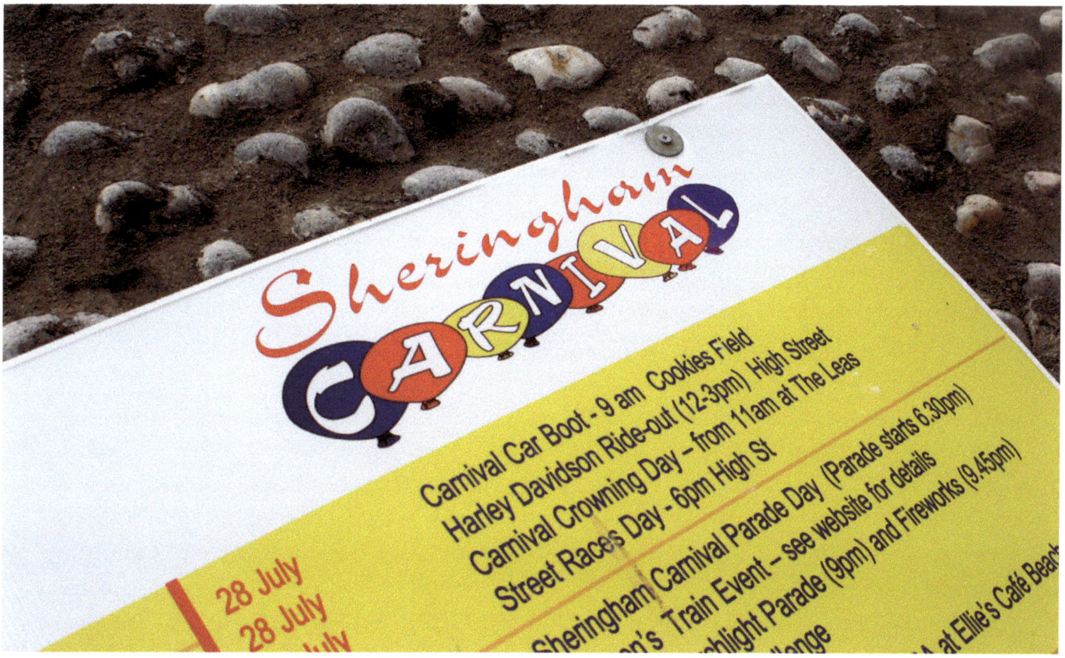

Sheringham and Cromer carnivals are a major source of entertainment.

would dive aflame from the pier to much applause from the audience. By the 1950s the carnival had grown and included a parade of floats that travelled through the town. The modern Cromer Carnival includes aerial entertainments like the Red Arrows and firework displays. Sheringham's carnival does not have such a long history but the week-long summer activities are a popular attraction. Sheringham also hosts a nostalgic 1940s weekend in the autumn, a morris dance weekend and, in the spring, a crab and lobster festival to celebrate all that is tasty about this valuable sea crop.

Cromer and Sheringham are well placed for people who enjoy outdoor pursuits. The North Norfolk Coast Path passes through both towns, making it a popular destination for walkers, and, as the North Sea gets more and more favoured by the surfing community, many visit to ride the waves. For others who like to get wet there is a designated snorkel trail in Sheringham. It follows the 150-foot length of a disused Victorian sewer pipe with ropes, buoys and information signs along the way, all of which are underwater.

Cromer and Sheringham have many golf courses. Edward VII was a founder member of the Royal Cromer Golf Club and he often played there, although, like most of the golf ranges in the area, the cliff edge location makes accuracy essential.

The actress Lillie Langtry, who was well known to Edward VII, played Sheringham's Little Theatre in 1906 and was one of the famous tourists to visit the resorts. The sea has inspired many, and composer Ralph Vaughn Williams lived in Sheringham during 1919, where he wrote his first major work *A Sea Symphony*. Sir Winston Churchill and his wife

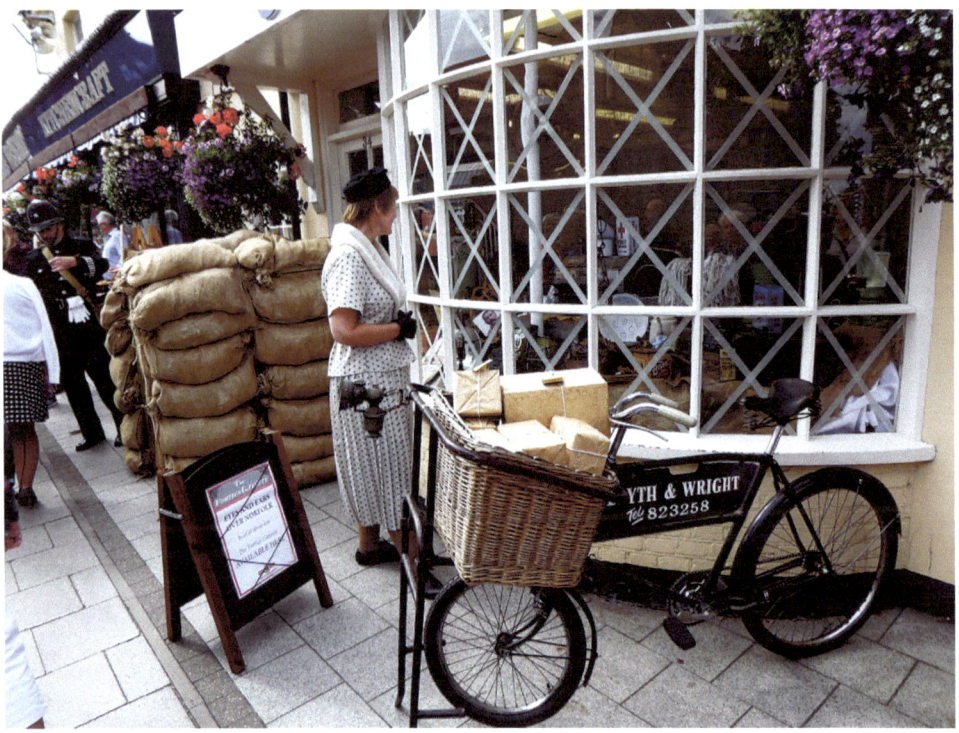

North Norfolk Railway hosts an annual 1940s weekend in Sheringham.

visited Cromer while he was on duty as First Lord of the Admiralty, and were so drawn to the sea and the pier that they became regular visitors.

The beauty of the region was famously written about by Clement Scott. A journalist, theatre critic and travel writer for the *Daily Telegraph*, he was completely beguiled by the area when he visited to do a newspaper article in 1883. The poems and prose he wrote about the place he called 'Poppy land' so impressed his readers that many of the theatre set with whom he mixed, Oscar Wilde and Tennyson among them, bought properties around Cromer and Sheringham. Scott later regretted writing about his love of 'Poppy land', saying he felt the mass of tourists his writings had brought to the area had ruined the peace and solitude he had originally found there.

Arthur Conan Doyle was another regular visitor and he is said to have used the local legend of Black Shuck as a basis for his Sherlock Holmes book *The Hound of the Baskervilles*. Conan Doyle stayed at Cromer Hall, a private Victorian residence, and used the look of this Tudor Gothic mansion for his realisation of Baskerville Hall. The hound itself he based on the legend of Black Shuck. Claimed to be the oldest phantom in the British Isles, Black Shuck has an Anglo-Saxon origin. Folklore tells of a colossal black dog with glowing eyes, prowling along the Sheringham to Cromer cliff path at night, stalking prey. If any unsuspecting walker should turn in the gloom and look into its eyes they will be dead within the year. There have, fortunately, been no reports of this ever happening.

Not all tourists experience this Gothic view of Cromer and Sheringham and instead enjoy the freedom and convenience of travel with a caravan. Covered wagons have been around for centuries but were only associated with itinerant workers, showmen and Romanies. In the late nineteenth century self-catering holidays became fashionable and by the twentieth century the idea of taking your own accommodation with you when

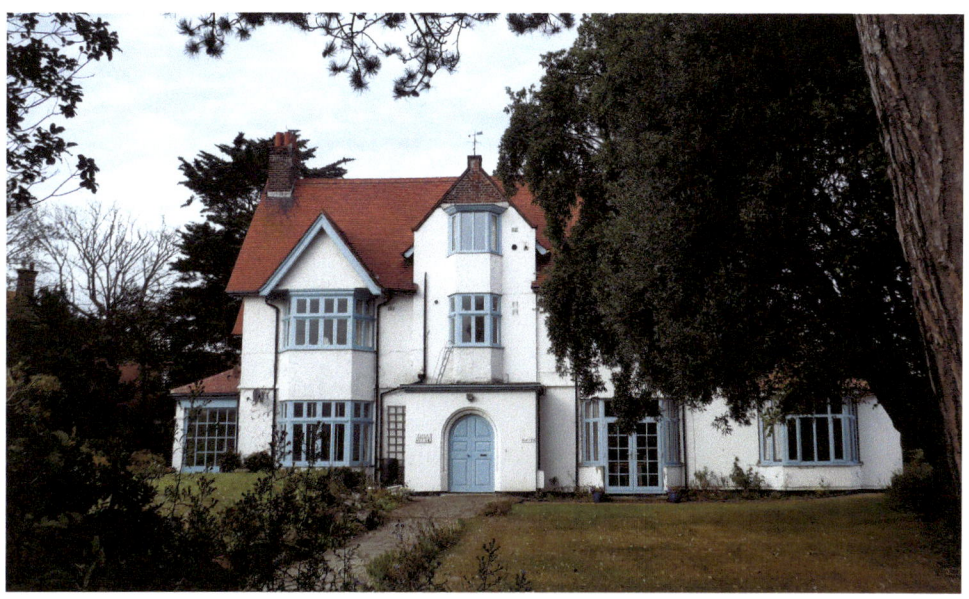

Composer Vaughn-Williams gained inspiration by living by the sea.

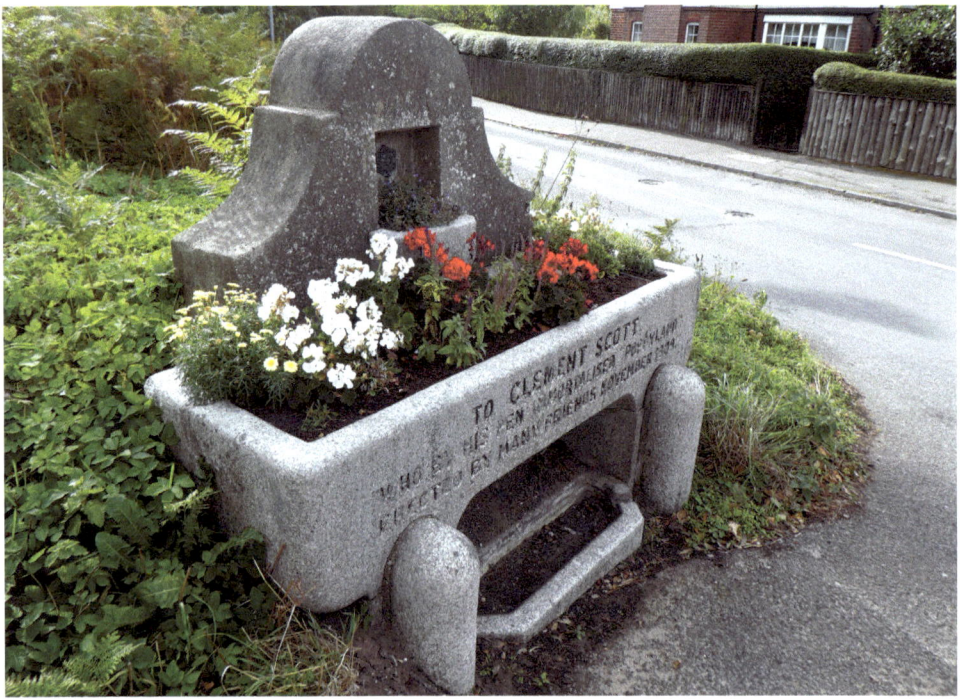

One of the writers to immortalise the area was Scott.

going on holiday started to evolve. The Camping and Caravanning Club was founded in 1907 and by 1919 caravans started to be pulled by the motor car. Seeing a potential new trade, farmers in Cromer and Sheringham began to rent out field space to accommodate this new type of holidaymaker.

In 1947 the government introduced paid annual leave for all workers and this allowed the working classes to enjoy an annual family holiday by the sea. These additional tourists needed somewhere to stay and the farmers who were renting out caravan spaces added static caravans to their sites as inexpensive holiday rentals. The caravan sites grew and although the route from Cromer to Sheringham is now lined with caravans, they are an important economic asset.

Tourists also add to the economy by purchasing souvenirs and taking a memento of their holiday home with them. Since Victorian times inexpensive items depicting Cromer and Sheringham have been produced for the tourist trade. The Victorian tourist believed in keeping up with fashion and as Cromer and Sheringham were extremely popular at the time, souvenirs on display in Victorian homes proved that the occupants had been to these very fashionable places. The town crest was a favourite ornamentation on small pieces of souvenir porcelain but as Cromer did not have its own crest, producers 'borrowed' the heraldic crest of the family name, Cromer, to use instead. Sheringham has its own town crest, which depicts two pinecones and a ship, illustrating the motto 'Twixt Sea and Pine'. An extreme souvenir of Cromer is in Australia. A town near Sydney changed its name to Cromer in 1940 after this gem of the Norfolk coast.

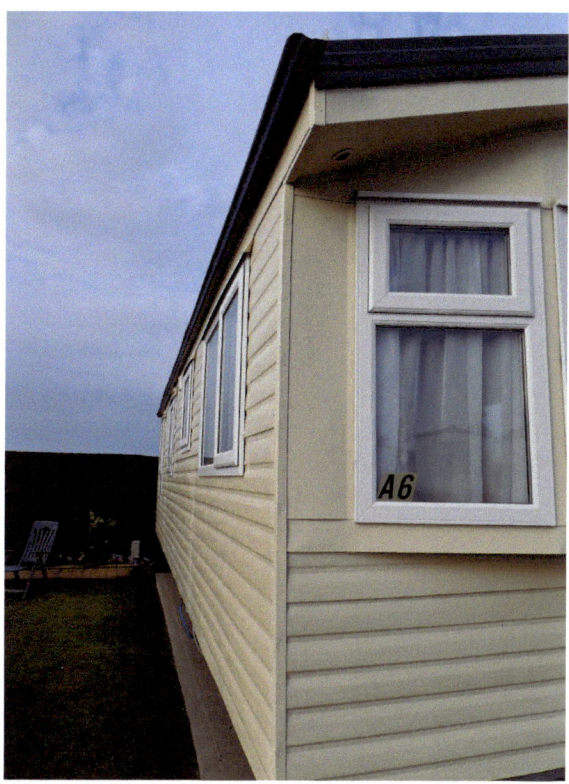

Caravans provide inexpensive holidays and plenty of fun.

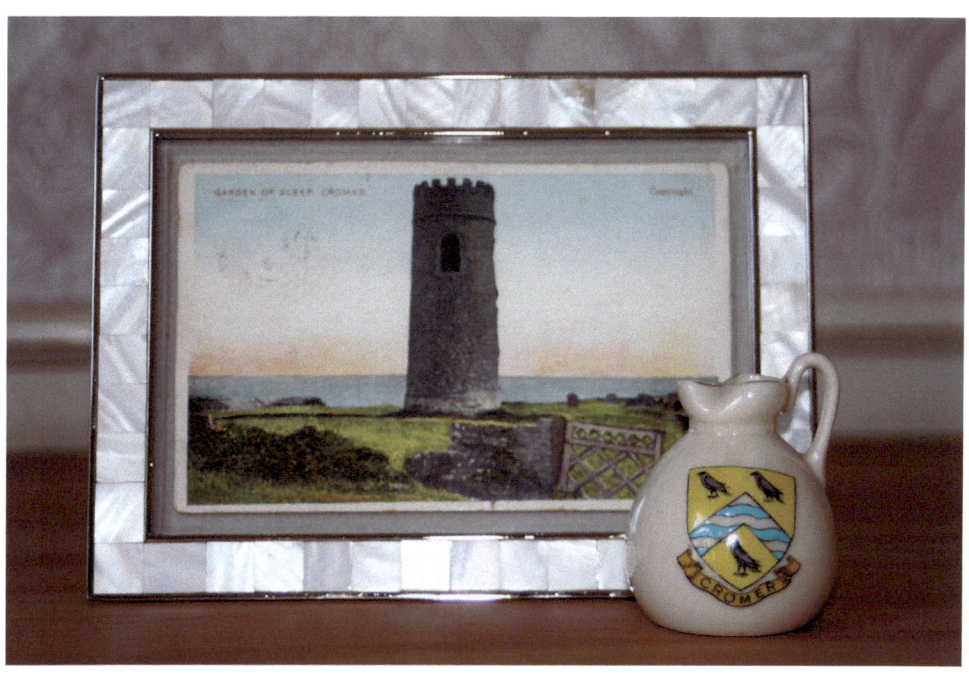

Holiday souvenirs were proudly displayed on Victorian mantlepieces.

5. The Anonymity of Philanthropy

Philanthropy, that selfless quality of giving of aid to others, often goes unnoticed and unrecognised. From a time before the Norman Conquest, large portions of land have been owned by those lucky enough to have money. The landowners allowed tenants to farm their land but raised high taxes on any produce, leaving little for the tenant farmer, who would be evicted the minute a crop failed and he could not pay. By the start of the Victorian era attitudes had changed and although there were still a lot of estates in the Cromer and Sheringham area that were owned by single large families, unlike the earlier lords of the manor these landowners had a genuine desire to help their tenants and those who lived on or around their land. They used their considerable wealth to benefit the community. Over the years many people have left their mark by providing for improvements to the local environment, but they are rarely recognised for their quiet contributions. The improvements, donations and gifts they have left have become a secret legacy.

The most recognised view of Sheringham is looking down the High Street to where the clock tower stands. This town clock was an Easter gift to Sheringham in 1903 by Mary Pym. The site used to be that of the old town stocks but became the main congregating area after it was discovered there was a spring there. The lower structure was built in 1862 to house a well and at that time it was the only water supply for the town. Each side had a drinking trough and locals used to carry the water home in pails slung over their shoulders, using apparatus similar to that carried by milkmaids. Mary Pym chose to put the clock over the spring because it was the main meeting place in Sheringham and, therefore, the maximum number of people would benefit from it. When a mains water supply was introduced, the spring and water troughs were no longer needed and the structure was altered to become a seating area. It is still a meeting place and focal point for the town.

The large clifftop car park in Cromer, which is crammed with visitors' vehicles every season, was provided through an act of benevolence by Mr R. W. Clarke. He donated the expanse of land for use by the town in whichever way it served them best and it was originally set out as a recreation field and playground for children. Over time, the needs of the people who lived in or visited Cromer changed, and the purpose of the field altered also. It went on to provide the car parking that was desperately needed by the town as the twentieth century progressed. A car park may not be the most attractive use for a plot of land, but it is vital to bring trade and prosperity to Cromer. Mr Clarke wished to benefit the town, and the car park does just that.

The family name of the Lords Suffield is Harbord, and these were a family of landowners whose generosity helped to shape Cromer. In the 1860s Lord Suffield, who had shares in the East Norfolk Rail Company, ensured the railway came to Cromer and Sheringham by allowing the company to cut straight across his land with the rail tracks.

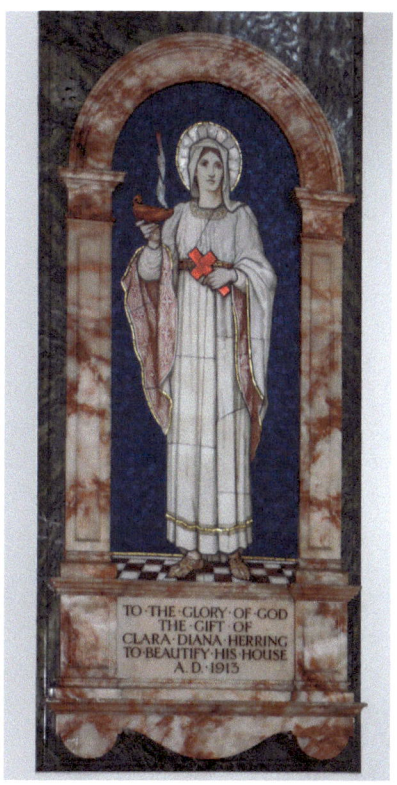

Many benefactors give small but beautiful gifts.

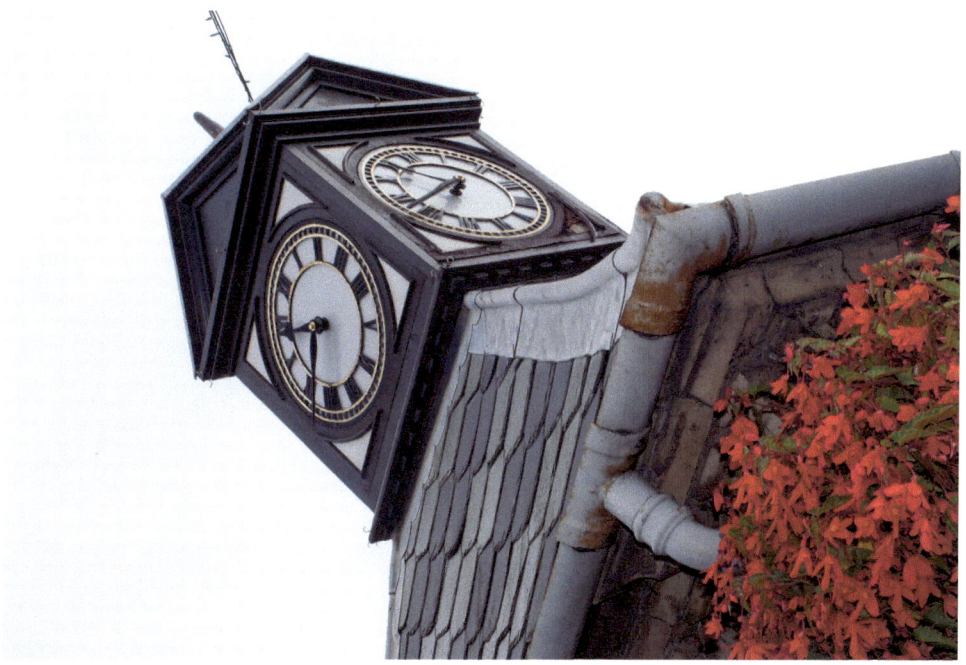

Sheringham town clock has always been a local meeting site.

He actively promoted the area to his peers and allowed his private house to be converted into a hotel to accommodate the many tourists he realised were valuable to the local economy. He was also influential in the introduction of the lifeboat service, which has since been responsible for saving thousands of lives.

Benjamin Bond Cabell was a Victorian philanthropist who donated a major part of his wealth to the lifeboat service and bought a lifeboat that was named after him. The boat served Cromer for many years. In Sheringham, major donors to their lifeboat service were the Upcher family. The family moved to Sheringham Park in 1811 and commissioned Sheringham Hall. Abbott Upcher was only thirty-five when he died and his wife, Charlotte, was devastated by his loss. Tragically, Charlotte's daughter died shortly afterwards and the bereft Charlotte dedicated the rest of her life to helping the people of Sheringham. She provided Sheringham's first lifeboat, named *Augusta* in memory of her daughter, and lent money to local fishermen to purchase new boats. Charlotte gave land for allotments, enabling families to grow their own produce, and set up a soup kitchen for those for whom times were really hard. All Saints Church in Upper Sheringham contains memorials to the Upcher family.

The magnificent Church of St Joseph in Sheringham was only built because a local resident provided funds for it. Mrs Kate Deterding was married to the managing director of the Royal Dutch Petroleum Company. When the couple moved to England they bought a large property on an estate near Sheringham. Kate wanted to give something to benefit the community she had become a part of and the town where she now, contentedly, lived. She approached the Catholic Church with the idea of creating a church that was as

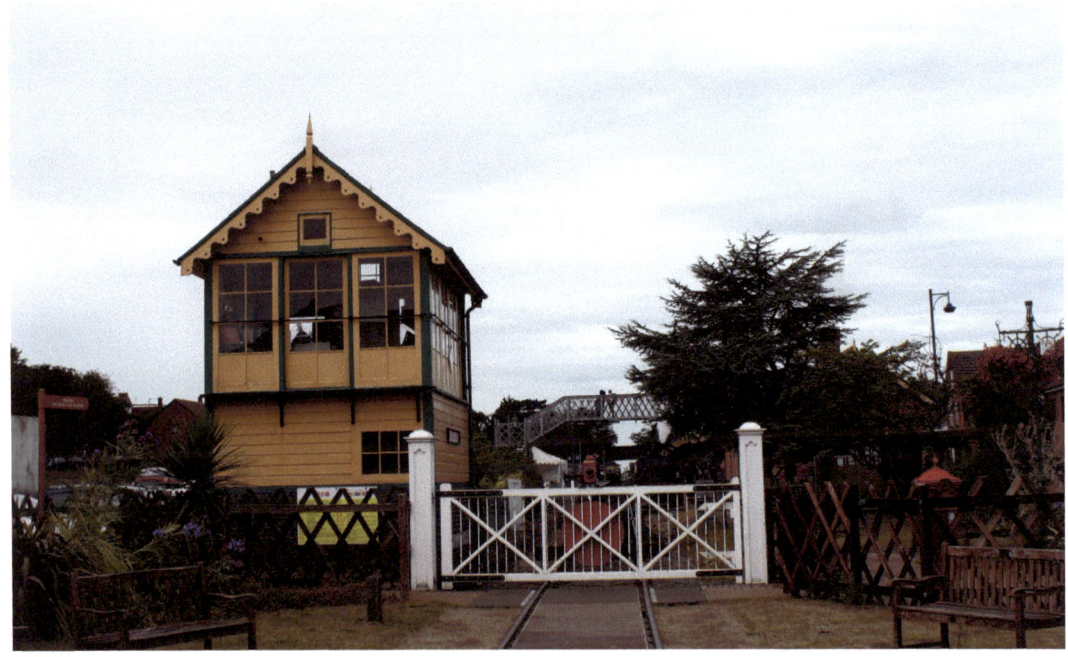

Railways brought the early tourists and now delight modern ones.

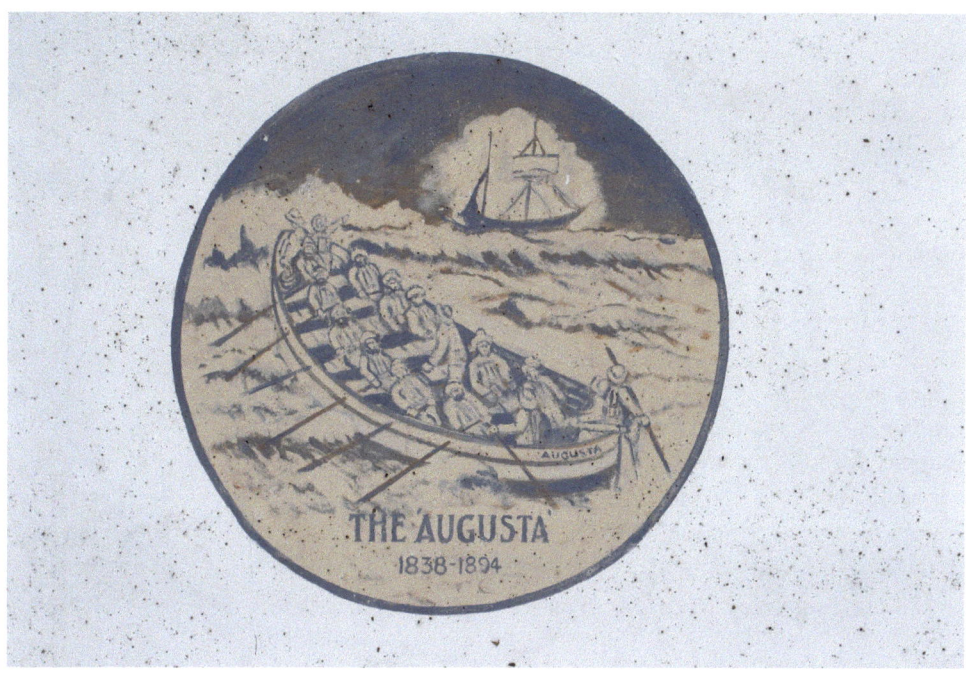

Sheringham's first lifeboat was donated in memory of Augusta Upcher.

grand as the new house she had recently moved into, and St Joseph's was subsequently commissioned. Mrs Deterding only converted to Catholicism just before her death in 1916 and is buried in St Joseph's.

DID YOU KNOW?
A rather unphilanthropic viewpoint was taken in 1650 when Cromer pier needed funds for repairs. This was in the middle of Cromwell's puritan era, when cathedrals were given no importance and power had switched from the bishop to the mayor of a city. It was suggested by the local council that Norwich Cathedral be demolished and any lead and useful materials be used to rebuild the pier. It was recorded that, 'Funds are short, and that vast and altogether useless cathedral has no other purpose.' The population's desire to have somewhere to pray was not taken into account.

Many wealthy banking families moved from Norwich to Cromer and Sheringham in the nineteenth century. These were the Gurneys, Buxtons, Barclays and Hoares, and they all happened to be Quakers with a strong belief in equality, pacifism and human rights. Their legacy has improved the lives of communities worldwide but a lot of their little

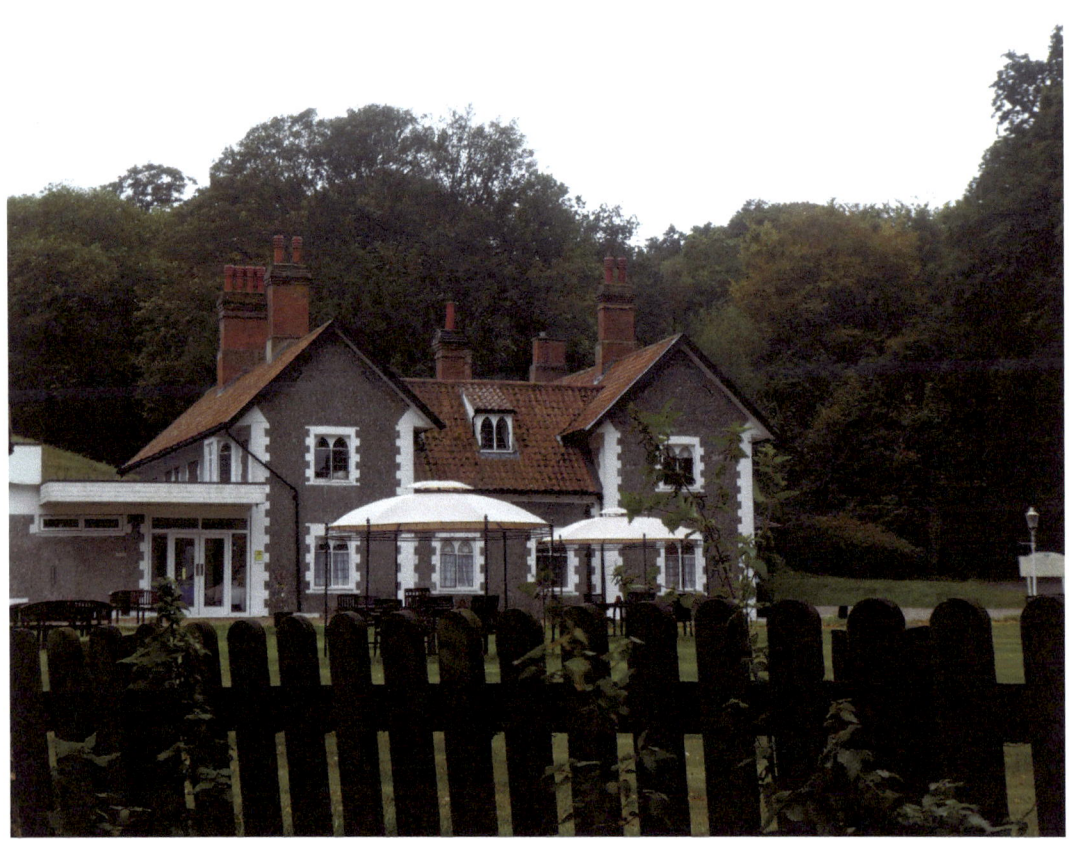

'The Cottage Ladies' actually lived in a grand house.

kindnesses benefitted Cromer and Sheringham. One member of the Gurney family was the prison reformer and abolitionist Elizabeth Fry. As well as campaigning in London, she looked after the welfare of the residents in her family's town and provided a reading room in Cromer for the use of all local fishermen. Elizabeth's cousins, Anna Gurney and Sarah Maria Buxton, were residents of Northrepps Cottage near Cromer and were always known locally as the 'Cottage Ladies'. They dedicated their lives to helping residents of the area as well as working with other reformers of the time to change working and living conditions countrywide. The cousins allowed their home to be used to educate the local children while Overstrand village school was being built, and the Cottage Ladies paid for the school's construction and staff. Anna, who was disabled and chair-bound, was an educated and spirited woman. She bought 'Manby's apparatus' for the lifeboat station to help save the lives of local seamen and fishermen. The apparatus fired a rocket attached to a lifeline as a way to reach a vessel in distress. Anna had researched the apparatus and understood better than most of the rescue team how the equipment worked. She insisted that she be carried to the beach when the rocket was launched so that she could personally oversee its use and help in any other way she could.

DID YOU KNOW?
The Upcher family of Sheringham has a memorial to them, other than those in their local church. Henry Morris Upcher also has a bird named after him. Upcher's Warbler is a native of Asia and had been discovered by a previous ornithologist, although the bird had remained unnamed and the description was said to be vague. Henry Baker Tristram, ornithologist and great friend of Henry Upcher, recategorised the tree warbler in clearer terms and named it Upcher's Warbler after his friend, who was renowned for his singing voice.

Philanthropy is still common. The large company that owns the Sheringham Shoal Wind Farm benefits financially from all the power that the elements produce. The company does not want to work in isolation out to sea but to invest in the local community as well. In 2010 the company set up the Sheringham Shoal Community Fund to benefit all of those living in the Sheringham area. The Shoal donates funds to many local causes involving maritime welfare or green energy issues.

Not all donations are large but all of them make a difference. Flower troughs and floral displays adorn both Cromer and Sheringham, and many people who enjoy the sight don't realise that they have been personally funded by local businesses and residents. Similarly, when North Lodge Park in Cromer was developed in the 1930s, local people donated shrubs, bushes and flowers to make it an attractive and welcoming place. The public benches, often dedicated to the memory of a loved one, that line the promenades of Sheringham and Cromer are provided by generous residents and visitors. They want to return the pleasure that they have, on previous occasions, gained themselves and donate a seat where anyone can stop, sit, relax and take in the serene atmosphere of the shoreline.

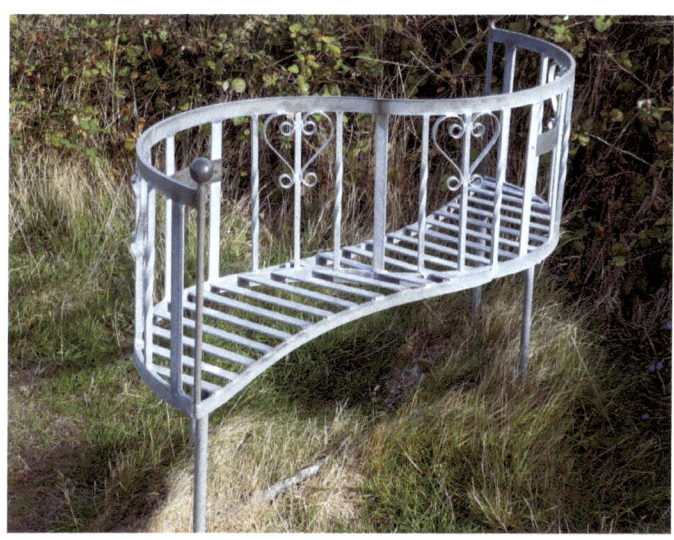

Everyone can sit and rest because others give generously.

6. The Untold Cost of War

Cromer and Sheringham have been protecting their communities from the aggression of others for millennia. The last actual invasion of Britain was the Norman Conquest in the eleventh century, and although since then the shores have been free of invading armies, conflict and fear have not disappeared. Self-protection and protecting those close to you are a human right, but if mankind had the humanity it thinks it has, wars would have ceased to exist by now. Sadly not so, and war continues to create a physical and emotional scar on all involved.

Both Cromer and Sheringham have war memorials to the fallen of the First World War and the Second World War and the quantity of names inscribed on them makes the emotional loss to local families painfully obvious. Not all lives were lost fighting overseas. Sheringham was the site of the first bomb ever dropped on mainland Britain from an aircraft. It was discharged by a Zeppelin in 1915, and although thankfully no one was killed on this occasion, the bombs that hit Cromer in 1942 were more catastrophic. Six members of the same family lost their lives in a single direct hit on their house.

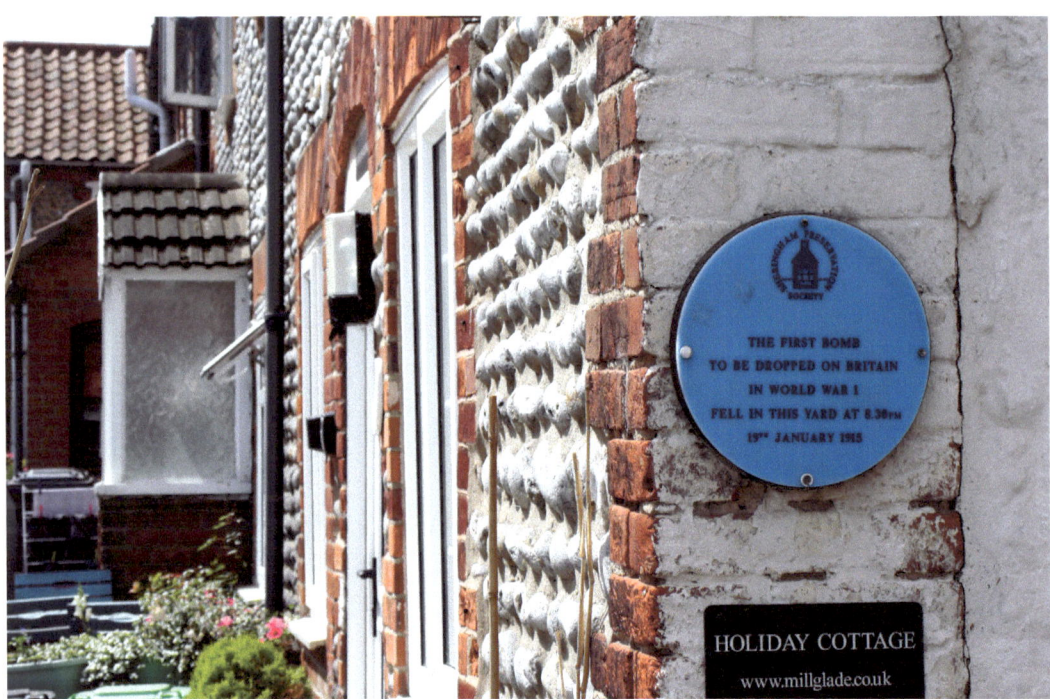

The site where the first bomb fell on British soil.

The environment is also affected by the threat, or reality, of war. It is altered through destructive acts by the enemy or the creation of defensive structures by the home troops. It is not always easy to tell which features of Cromer and Sheringham are a reminder of conflict, but the gap in a parade of shops or the newer house in the middle of a terraced street tell their tale of bomb damage, and the random red-brick ruin in the middle of the beach is not a garden ornament slipped from the cliff but the remains of an anti-aircraft gun turret from the Second World War.

Cromer and Sheringham have always been considered particularly vulnerable to invading armies as the steep gradient of the beach, especially at Weybourne, could allow enemy vessels to get dangerously close to the shore. When the threat came from the Spanish Armada in the 1580s, plans were being discussed for a defensive fort to be built on Weybourne Cliffs. Although the fort was never built, the cliffs had trenches dug into them, making it difficult for enemy troops to leave the beaches in the event they managed to disembark, and sea gulleys were blocked to prevent the enemy from getting inland by water. The towns of Cromer and Sheringham were both equipped with some form of munitions as further protection in the event of invasion. Evidence of these can be seen in Sheringham, where the barrel of a gun still leans nonchalantly against a wall at the top of Gun Street. During the time of the Spanish Armada the gun was at the other end of this street, pointing out to sea and ready to fire on any approaching enemy ships. Cromer was provided with two similar guns that guarded the sea from the point by the pier where the Hotel de Paris now stands.

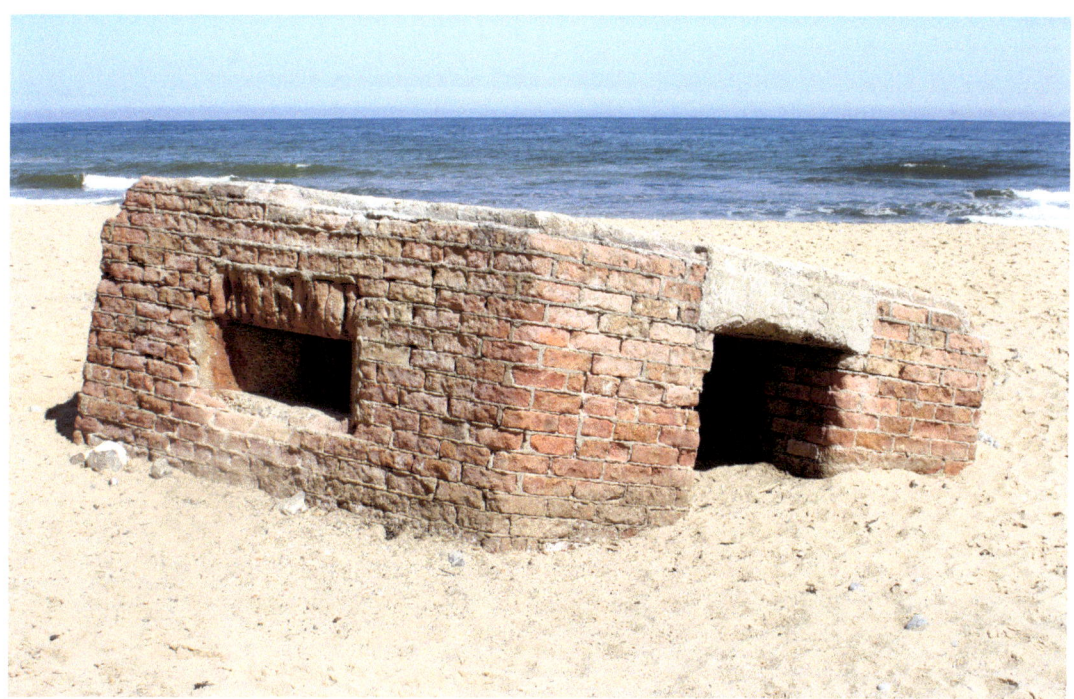

Many reminders of the Second World War remain on the beaches.

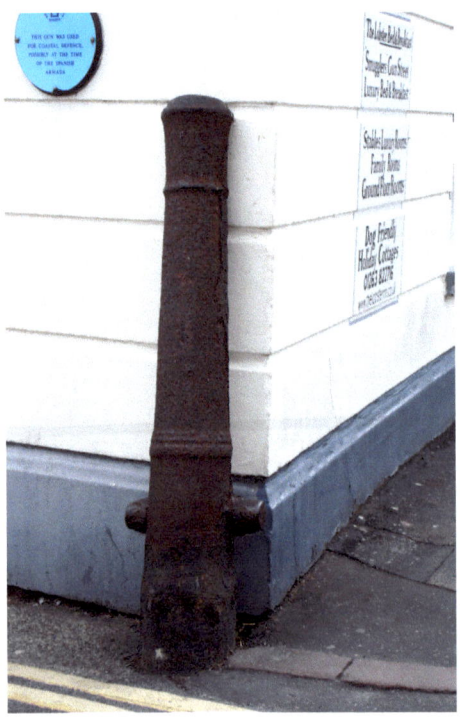

The gun in Sheringham dates back to the Spanish Armada.

These invasion fears proved unfounded, but coastal towns like Cromer and Sheringham heightened their defensive measures when the Napoleonic Wars started, and the area was readied for the war to come. Many sea battles took place off the coast and it was necessary to strengthen the gun defences at Cromer and Sheringham with the addition of cannon. The fear of French invasion was so great that the king ordered a scorched earth policy. The policy stated that, 'Should any French troops make it to shore, there must be total destruction of any resources in their path deemed useful to the enemy, whether food, shelter, arms or equipment.' A merchant shipping convoy was mistakenly identified as the French fleet by a Cromer lookout and he rushed to raise the alarm. Fortunately, his mistake was realised before military forces proceeded to employ the scorched earth solution or many farms, food stores and buildings around Cromer and Sheringham would have been lost.

The navy needed more and more men to fight in the Napoleonic Wars. Men of Sheringham and Cromer had already volunteered as local infantry and they stood as an eighty-strong force ready to be called on in case of invasion near the towns. However, navy ships needed manning urgently and any men in the area with no fixed abode were forced into service. This was known as press ganging and would continue well into the nineteenth century. Men down on their luck who became infantry men or sailors often died in appalling conditions. The twentieth century brought a change of attitude to recruitment, and when the call-up for the First World War began there was no shortage of volunteers. Hundreds of young men left 'Poppy land' to fight for their country on the alternative fields of poppies in France.

DID YOU KNOW?
During the Zeppelin raids of the First World War, Sheringham was the unfortunate target of the first bombs dropped on British soil. One bomb fell straight through the roof of a cottage in the town and was detonated. The quick-thinking occupant grabbed the incendiary device, rushed outside and dropped it in a horse trough to extinguish it. This prevented major damage and casualties and the bomb is now on display in Sheringham museum.

In 1914, both Sheringham and Cromer had an optimistic belief that life would go on as usual. Domestic life initially had its normal routine but, in 1915, the German Zeppelin raids began in an attempt to break British morale. Sheringham, infamously, was the target for the first bomb dropped on Britain. The town, sadly, suffered other strikes as it lay on the flight path to Kings Lynn. After this bombing, the tourist trade disappeared and life completely changed for the remaining residents.

One in four men had gone off to fight and, as the tourists had ceased to visit, the population of Sheringham and Cromer seemed depleted. However, the area had become a venue for training and stationing troops and these new visitors started to arrive. The residents of Cromer and Sheringham had an unsettled relationship with the soldiers. The high streets were overcrowded with uniformed troops and military horses were

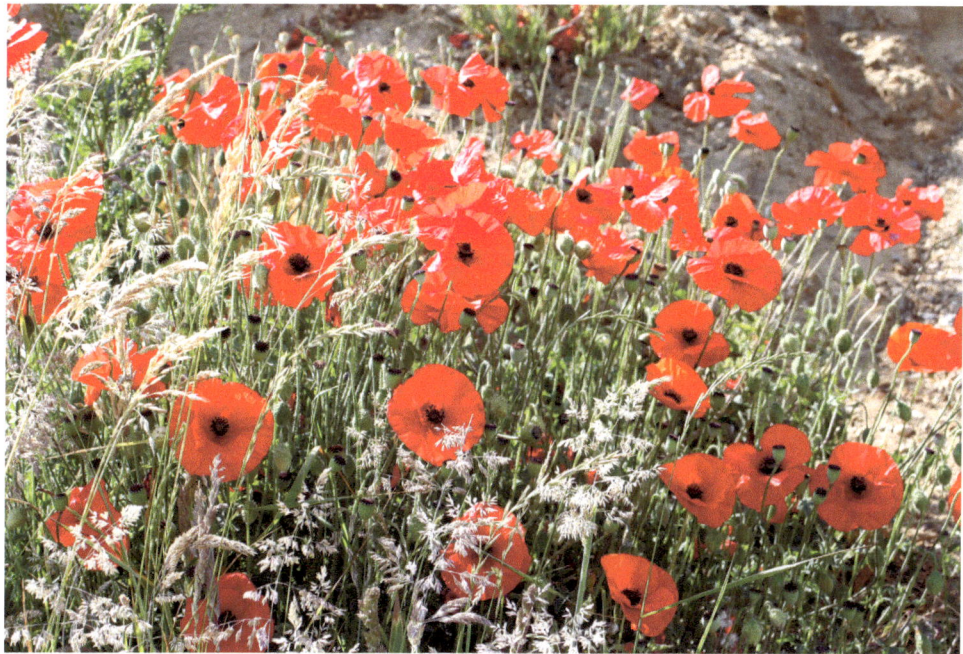

First World War volunteers left behind the poppies of home.

watered at the drinking troughs. There were guns placed throughout the towns to defend from attack by air or sea, but local residents reported that these were incapable of firing properly. They felt the presence of the soldiers invited attack from the enemy and actually put the town in more danger than if they had been left to fend for themselves. The troops brought trade, however, and many hotels and holiday residences were requisitioned for the billeting of military personnel. The service men filled the pubs and cafés, replacing the income lost when the tourists had ceased to visit, and this ensured a lot of local businesses managed to survive.

The headland at Foulness, where the Cromer Lighthouse is situated, was used as practise areas for trench digging in a vain attempt to ready the men for the conditions they would experience in France. There were so many incomers that churches could not accommodate all the extra worshippers and local hotel ballrooms and village halls had to be used for Sunday worship.

As so many men had enlisted, often due to encouragement from the women, it became the women's role to do as much as they could for the war effort at home. Edith Upcher and other wealthy ladies put a lot of effort into helping their country. They worked as volunteer auxiliary nurses in local hospitals and Edith helped set up a field dressing depot to ensure medical supplies got to military hospitals in Britain and also on the front line. The fishermen had gone to war and fishing was not possible due to the presence of soldiers on the beach, so a lot of the women from fishing families in both Cromer and

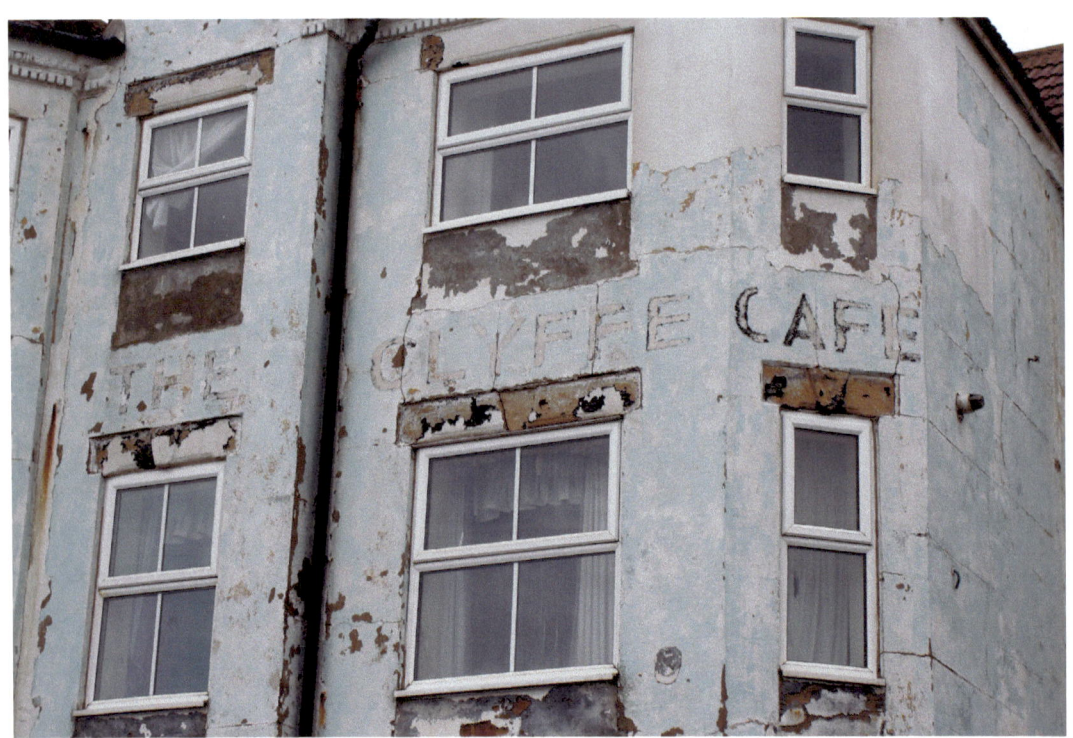

Hotels were used to billet the military during both wars.

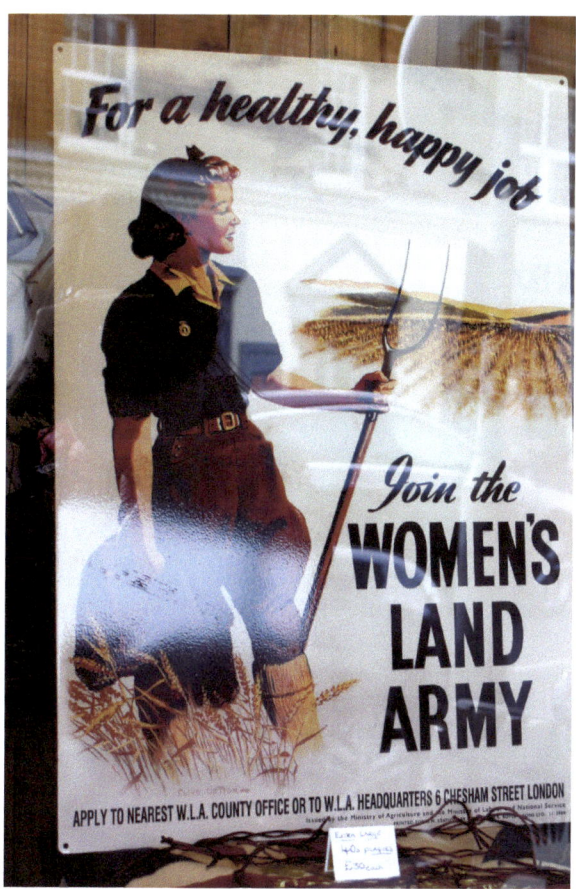

Every woman did what she could on the home front.

Sheringham turned their hands to working the land. The war office demanded that land was put aside to be ploughed and planted and provide a necessary source of home-grown food. Thirteen acres of the Royal Cromer Golf Course was ploughed up but the club was allowed to keep nine of its holes intact for use by the army officers. The green keepers, who had worked tirelessly to keep the course pristine, went off to fight.

DID YOU KNOW?
Throughout the Second World War, in an attempt to confuse any invasion force who may not have known exactly where they were after landing, any public sign displaying a place name had to be removed by law. On Sheringham Promenade, by the West End slipway, was, until recently, a pre-war right-of-way notice. The name Sheringham had clearly been chiselled off as a means of obliterating the town's identity. The cast-iron sign was firmly attached to the wall with rusty screws and it was seemingly considered too difficult to remove at the time.

Danger also came from friendly fire. When a mine drifted in towards shore at Sheringham, none of the military personnel knew how to stop it and the mine hit land and exploded on the beach. Remarkably, no one was injured, despite beach stones and shrapnel being thrown well into the town. Ever resilient, the Sheringham residents went around collecting metal shards from the mine so that they could prove it was British and claim compensation from the war office for any damage done.

Olive Edis was a talented photographer from Sheringham who experienced life on the home front and life in the trenches. Her career started in 1905 and she was a pioneer of early autochrome colour photography. Olive took photographs of Sheringham and Cromer fishermen and turned them into tourist postcards, making the sitters for these shots minor celebrities. However, it was her photography in the aftermath of battle that made Olive famous. She was made an official war photographer and went to France in 1918, and many of the photographs she took were used in later publications. Olive died in 1955 and is laid to rest in Sheringham cemetery. She is remembered through her photography, and many of those Olive photographed in France died on the battlefield and have no memorial at all.

The First World War was still a recent memory when, in 1939, the Second World War began. Life had settled back into a normal pattern after 1918 but now Cromer and Sheringham residents realised that life was going to change for them all over again.

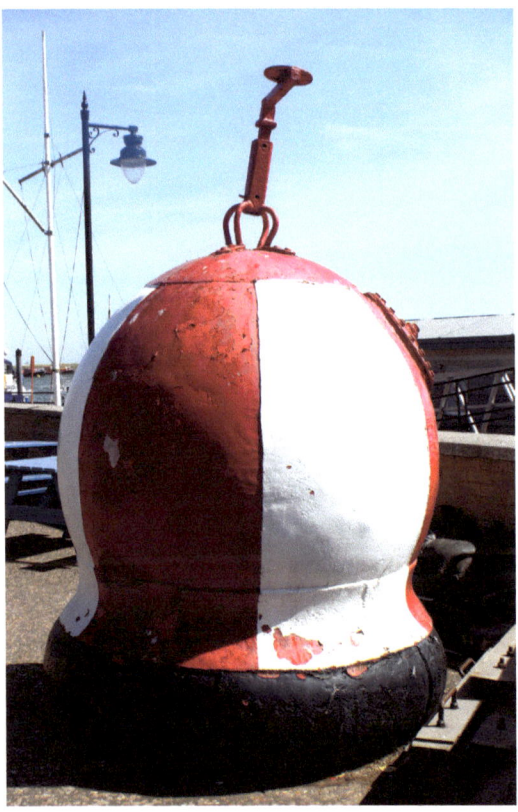

Mines were ever present along the wartime shore.

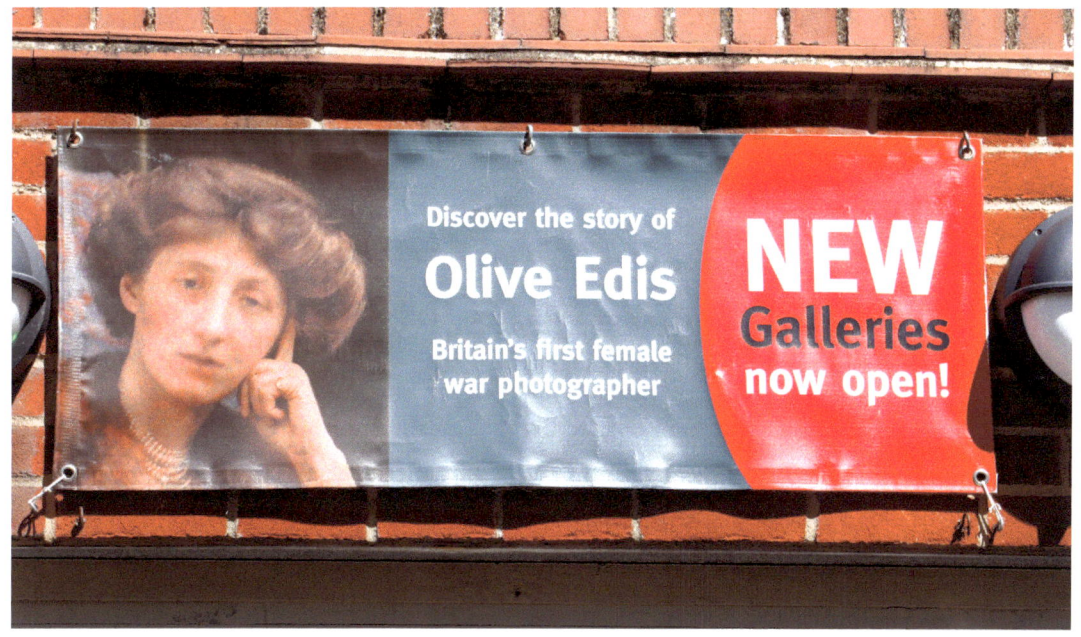

Olive Edis photographed a lot of First World War France.

At the beginning of the Easter season in 1940 Cromer and Sheringham had a surprising number of holidaymakers, but the pretence of normality did not last for long. In June that year it was made an offence for anyone to visit the seaside resorts for holidaying, pleasure or as a casual visitor. The strong military presence in the area made this a necessity for national security but not everyone realised that the town was out of bounds. Two elderly ladies were fined for ignoring the ruling after they had arrived in Cromer on a bus hoping to visit the pier. The bus company was also fined, as it too had broken the law by selling them the tickets in the first place.

Cromer and Sheringham residents had to rally together during times of war and crisis and this created a bond between the towns' people. However, as much as conflict created camaraderie, it also bred suspicion. An unknown individual was a potential enemy and a trusted friend could be capable of betrayal. Fear came with the appearance of strangers. The tourist industry had vanished, so anyone non-military checking into a hotel was viewed with distrust. When two respectable-looking women arrived in Sheringham, rumours started that they were spies and they were treated with hostility everywhere they went. It later turned out that they were two army wives waiting for their husbands to get leave, but this was only disclosed after days of verbal abuse. Similarly, when a lifeboat did not come back after a rescue as quickly as usual, it was said the Germans had captured their vessel. When the lifeboat arrived back in Sheringham, an unscheduled landing in Grimsby accounting for the delay, the crew was under suspicion. For weeks afterwards, some residents were convinced that the lifeboat men had become enemy spies. However, not all residents treated others with hostility and most people realised that everyone had their own part to play in supporting the war effort.

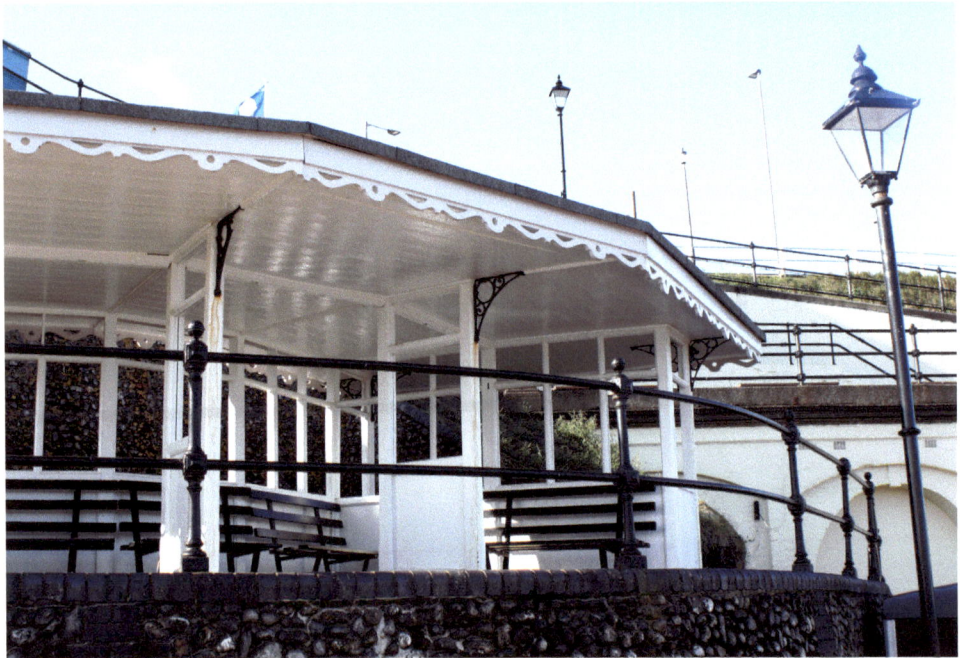

Wartime tourist areas were deserted and strangers caused concern.

In 1938 there had been a massive recruitment drive by the Sheringham and Cromer councils to get men to volunteer for the Territorial Army. Many men signed up and after the war started, and with it the formation of the Home Guard, this service too was inundated with volunteers. Many hundreds of men in the Cromer and Sheringham district who were not eligible to fight supported their country with tireless work on home soil.

When the plea came for boats to go to France to help with the evacuation of Dunkirk, the crew of every fishing boat in Sheringham volunteered, but most were too small and only two were allowed to go. These two boats and their crew travelled down the coast towards Folkestone but were turned back for being underpowered. In Cromer, the lifeboat crew was the first to volunteer to help at Dunkirk but, again, both this and the towns fishing boats were refused. The lifeboat was large and powerful enough to complete the mission but it was more important that it stay at home where it was frequently needed. Another challenge for the crew of the lifeboat occurred in 1940 when they lost access to their lifeboat station.

The station has been sited at the end of the pier since 1923 to make the launch of the lifeboat as efficient as possible. The military decided that it was necessary to remove the middle section of the pier in case enemy troops landed at Cromer. This was despite public opinion that it was ridiculous to expect the enemy to queue up to actually land on the pier itself. The pier was wired with explosives and due to be detonated at noon. All Cromer residents were advised to leave their windows open to prevent blast damage. No explosion happened and, as the weather was not good, everyone closed their windows

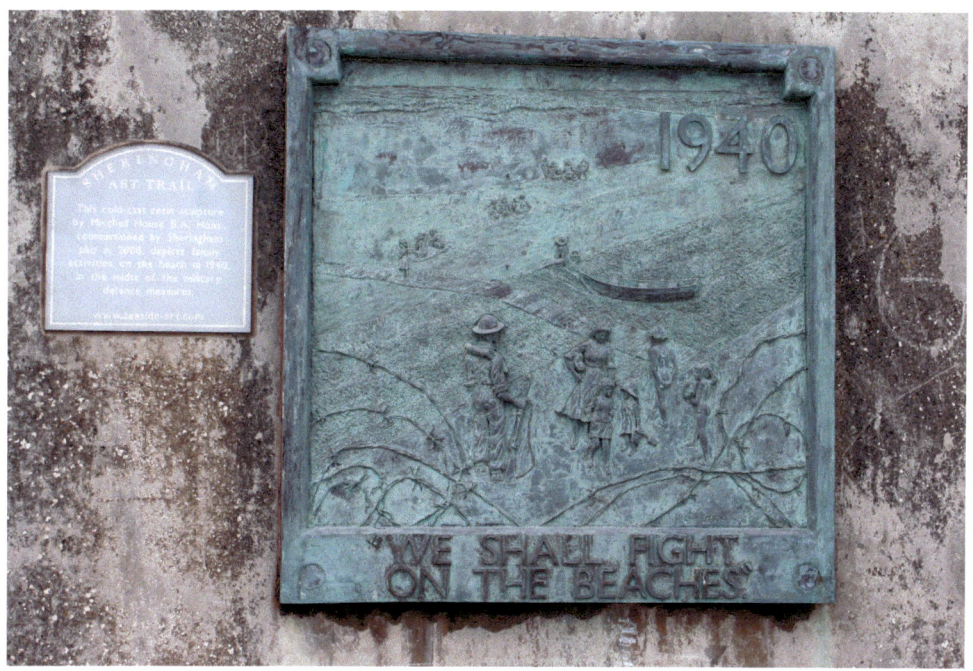

Every boat from both Cromer and Sheringham volunteered for Dunkirk.

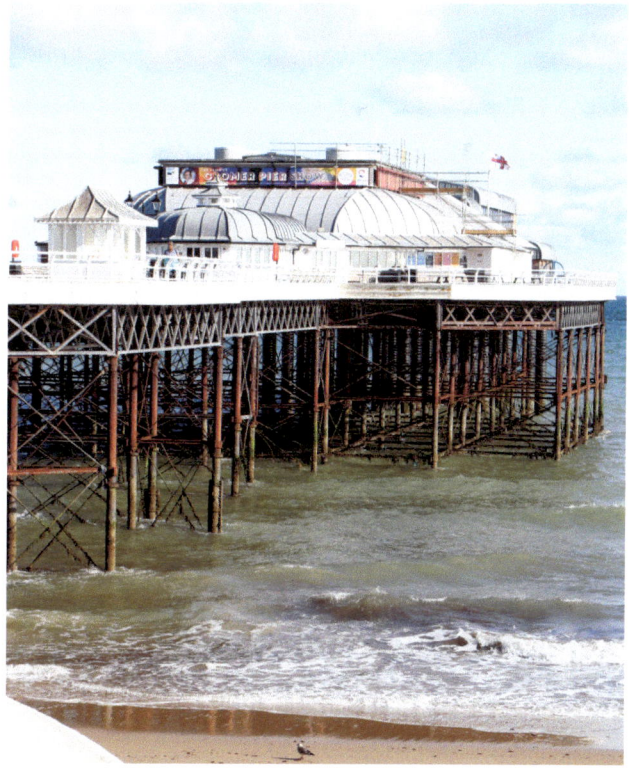

The central pier was breached
to preserve national security.

again by the middle of the afternoon. The detonation came unexpectedly at teatime, windows shattered and wreckage from the pier was blasted into the town. Fortunately, it caused no injuries. It was only when the pier stood in two halves that the military realised that the lifeboatmen couldn't access their lifeboat station. Rudimentary planking was hastily nailed across. This was both slippery and dangerous for the lifeboatmen and, ironically, reinstated access into the town via the pier for any invasion forces.

The holiday beaches were closed off by barbed wire, mines were anchored a little way out to sea and fishing was halted around Cromer and Sheringham due to the danger from shells discharged in gunnery practise at Weybourne camp. This gun practise was later stopped when it was discovered that the explosions were destabilising the already fragile cliffs. The mines had a tendency to explode with no warning and were moved from deep water, where the high tides meant the weight of water on the mine caused its detonation, to the sand above the tide line. Sadly, the mines went on to claim the lives of servicemen even after the war had ended. Mine clearing around the beaches was an ongoing and dangerous task. The last mines were not finally removed near Sheringham and Cromer until 1953, and twenty-six sappers died in making the area safe once more.

At the beginning of the war over 1,200 children from London were evacuated to the Cromer and Sheringham area. When the London evacuees arrived in 1939 the influx of children was so high that the local schools could not find room for everyone. A system was hastily developed to teach the local children in the morning and have another set

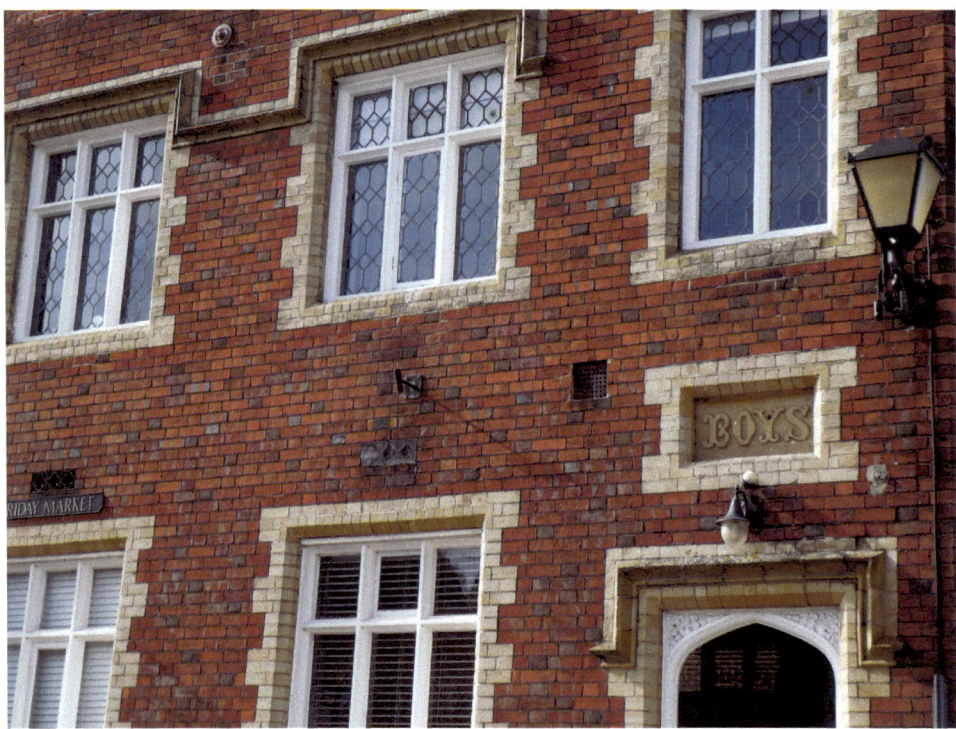

There were too many evacuees to teach in local schools.

of lessons for the evacuees in the afternoon. Local people were unsure of the London children, who had a much different life in the capital to that of the coast dwellers, and any petty thefts or trouble in the area was blamed on the evacuees. When the children's parents came to visit, some locals described them as 'common and uncouth'. Within a year, however, these children were evacuated again, away from Sheringham and Cromer to somewhere considered safer. Some residents felt relief when the evacuees had to leave, but most realised that it meant the towns were now recognised as being a high risk for enemy attack.

DID YOU KNOW?
Sheringham had a Second World War mystery. Small tin foil packets of yellow powder were found littering the town. Amid rumours of gas powder or poison dropped from enemy aircraft, they were removed by the military for testing. Meanwhile, the truth emerged. A hairdresser had let boy scouts collect the tin foil packets to reuse the foil, but wanted the contents emptying out. The lads decided it was too much trouble and had more fun aiming the packets at targets and making a mess. The powder was hair bleach and the scouts were very embarrassed at the worry they caused.

Although only two small seaside towns, air raids in Cromer and Sheringham became a very real event. Their coastal location near the military camp at Weybourne and intelligence station at Beeston made them unfortunate targets. Residents were provided with both Anderson shelters for their gardens, and Morrison shelters for indoor use. Communal air-raid shelters were also created, but these could not protect everyone or prevent property from being destroyed. The worst bombing raids were during July 1942. Eleven people lost their lives in Cromer on one night, countless buildings were destroyed and Cromer parish church was badly damaged. The war had a vast emotional effect on the people of Sheringham and Cromer. Telegrams addressed to families telling of lost or missing relatives became commonplace, and the death toll from air attacks in the towns grew.

One bomb tragically killed a young Cromer girl in her bed. Poignantly remembering the evening before the event, the child's mother told the local newspaper about a conversation between her daughter and herself. The child, who was called Doris, asked her mother, 'Is it true that if a bomb has your name on it, it is going to kill you?' Her mother replied, 'No bombs will ever have your name on, Sweetheart, and with a royal name like ours no-one would dare hurt any of us.' Doris King was killed by the bomb that struck their house that night. One local widow, Mrs Smith, was totally moved by the newspaper report. To help the war effort she, like many others, had been knitting for the troops. Mrs Smith donated a scarf that was received by a young airman and he sent her a thank you note. In it, he explained that in gratitude for her gift, he would write Mrs Smith's name on one the next

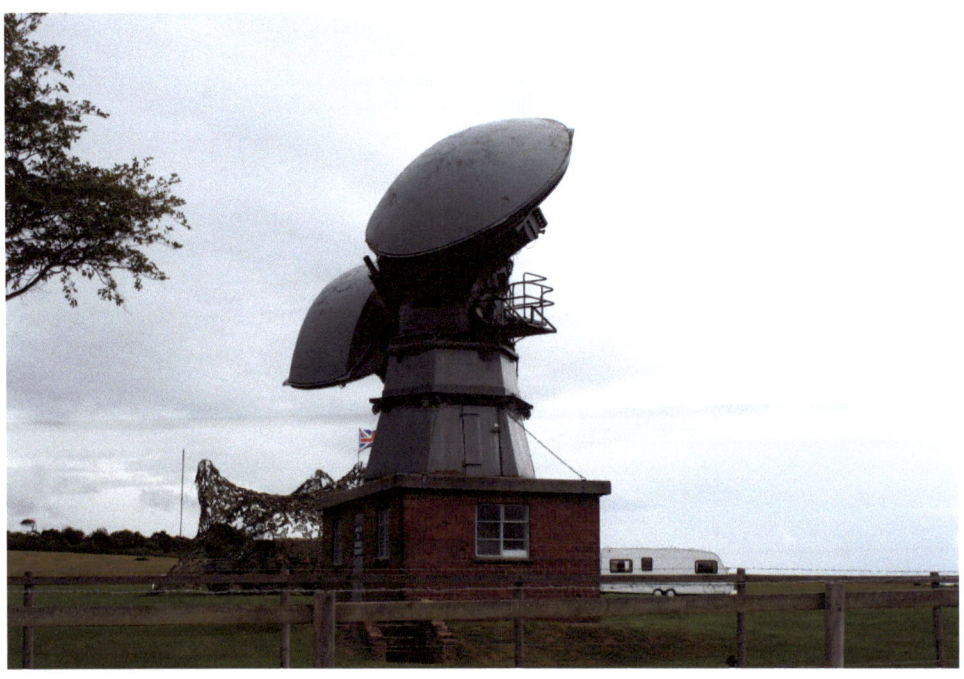

Their proximity to military sites made Sheringham and Cromer targets.

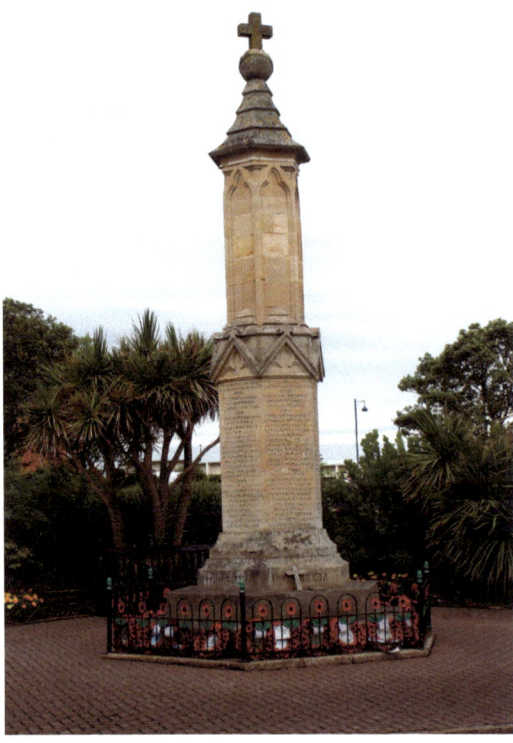

Sheringham war memorial stands as testament to many lost lives.

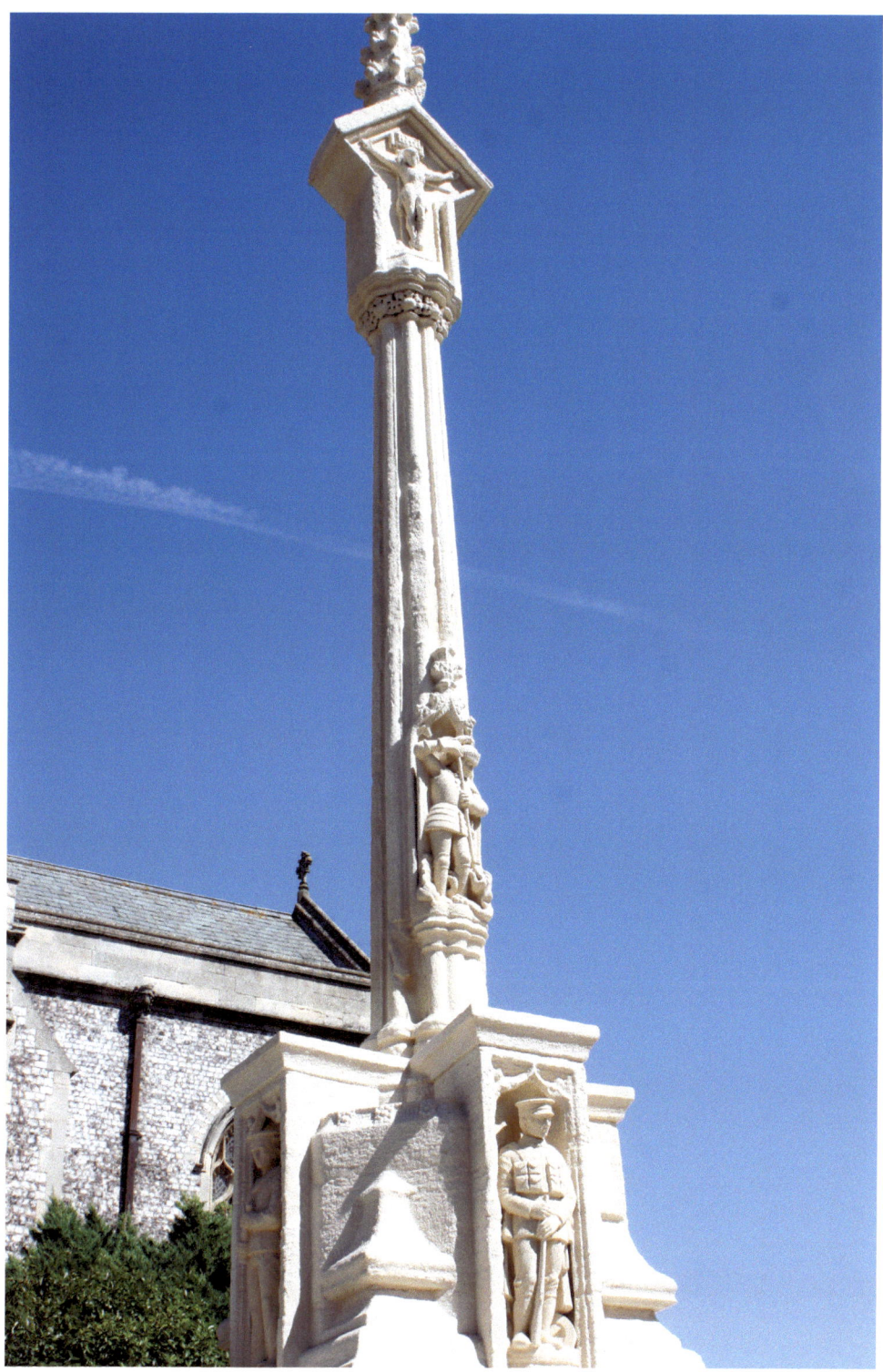

The war memorial in Cromer survived a devastating air raid.

bombs he dropped on Germany and she could then be there with him, helping to win the war. Mrs Smith sent the newspaper report about Doris King to his base, and firmly pointed out that winning the war did not mean the destruction of faceless foreigners, but the painful loss of real people with real lives.

Many years have passed since the end of the Second World War but there are still reminders all over Cromer and Sheringham. The beaches between the two towns will reveal the skeleton remains of pill box defences when the tide is out, and the bases of machine gun turrets are still on cliff tops. Concrete tank traps have been reused and are now unrecognisable, as they form a part of vital sea defences. High streets have been irreparably changed as entire hotels and shops were razed to the ground and never replaced, leaving only empty spaces. The west window in the Church of St Peter and St Paul in Cromer was destroyed by a bomb and the shop next to the church was destroyed in the same blast. The window was later replaced with the magnificent Ascension Window and the site of the shop has become a memorial garden. There is a poignancy to the fact that the memorial in the churchyard to the First World War withstood the bomb.

Inside the church, too, are memories of war. Revd Barclay was vicar from 1939 to 1946 and a commemorative plaque on the wall is to his two sons. Both were killed in action during the Second World War. On other rolls of honour are more recent dates. A testament to the fact that the men and women of Cromer and Sheringham are still being lost in conflicts worldwide.

7. Behind the Healthy Society

Cromer and Sheringham exist because of their proximity to the sea. The sea has provided food from its harvest of fish, and wealth from attracting visitors who enjoy the waves and invigorating air. Yet, as much as the sea encourages a feeling of health and well-being, it is also essential that those close to the water are protected from its dangerous elements. To keep the residents safe there have to be measures in place to defend against the environment, lives and shipping would be at risk without the coastguard, lifeboats and lighthouses. Not all emergency services are directly linked to the sea; hospitals and healthcare systems also look after the well-being of Cromer and Sheringham residents, and each one of these emergency services harbours an interesting and surprising origin.

The desire to explore the health-giving properties of seawater and fresh salty air became a fashion trend in the eighteenth century. In 1796, John Green, a journalist from London, recorded in his diary: 'Having suffered jaundice these last months, my doctor has ordered me to the sea and Cromer is the best place I can think of.' Recommendations like this promoted Cromer and Sheringham, tourists started to arrive for sea bathing and this became the first provision by the towns to the health and well-being of the population.

The Bath House stands on Cromer seafront and was built in 1814. In an attempt to rival inland spa towns like Bath or Buxton, the building had salt water pumped up from the sea into its private bath rooms. Wealthy gentlemen could bathe in seawater in total privacy and also receive other water treatments. Cromer soft drinks manufacturer Everetts even supplied the Bath House with its own local spring water.

It was considered unseemly to swim where you could be seen by someone of the opposite gender and to preserve the dignity of those wishing to enjoy the sea, the bathing machine was developed. This was a small, barrel-roofed covered cart that was taken from the top of the beach and down into the sea. The ladies and gentlemen changed into their swimwear in the bathing machine and could modestly enter the water to swim. The bathing machine hid the swimmer from view. The first bathing machines in Cromer appeared in 1779. They were operated by Dr Sidney Terry, a hydrotherapist, who promoted them as, 'a means for conveniently conveying gentlefolk, confidentially, to their swim.'

The need for the bathing machine waned in the twentieth century, when the onset of the Edwardian era heralded a more relaxed view on acceptable conduct. By 1912, bathing machines were considered old fashioned and out of date and Sheringham and Cromer replaced them with the permanent beach huts that have been a feature of the promenades ever since.

A natural resource that has always appeared in varying degrees in Great Britain, but still caused tourists to flock to Cromer and Sheringham for health reasons, was sunshine. Between the 1920s and the 1980s the desire for a deep suntan was absolute. In the 1920s medical proof emerged that sunlight promoted the production of vitamin D and it

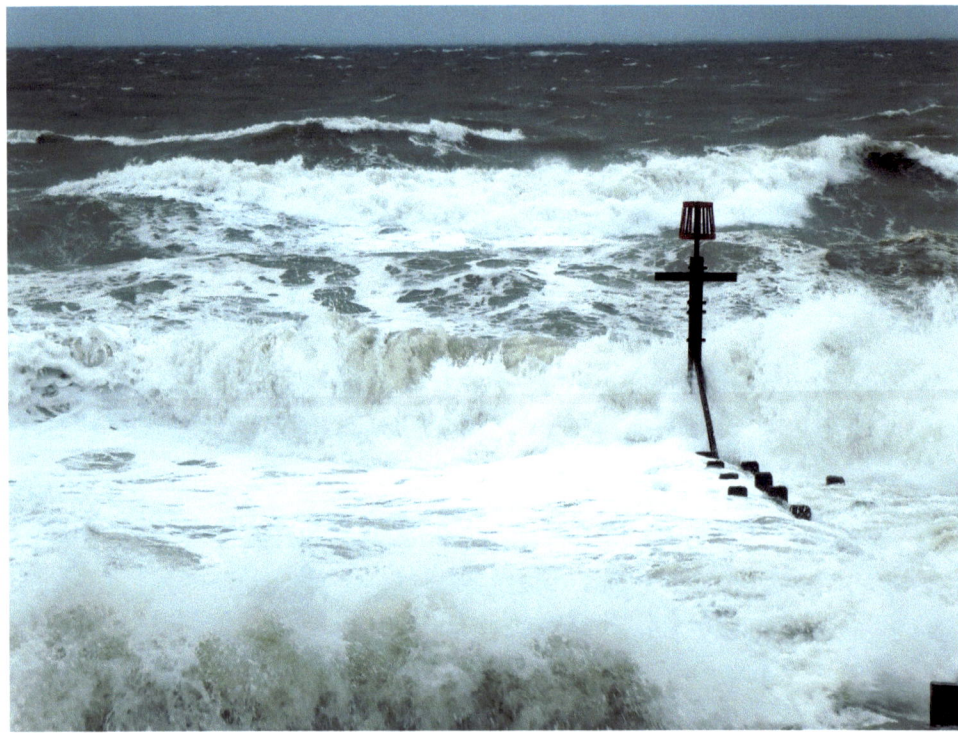

The sea brings in a livelihood but also brings danger.

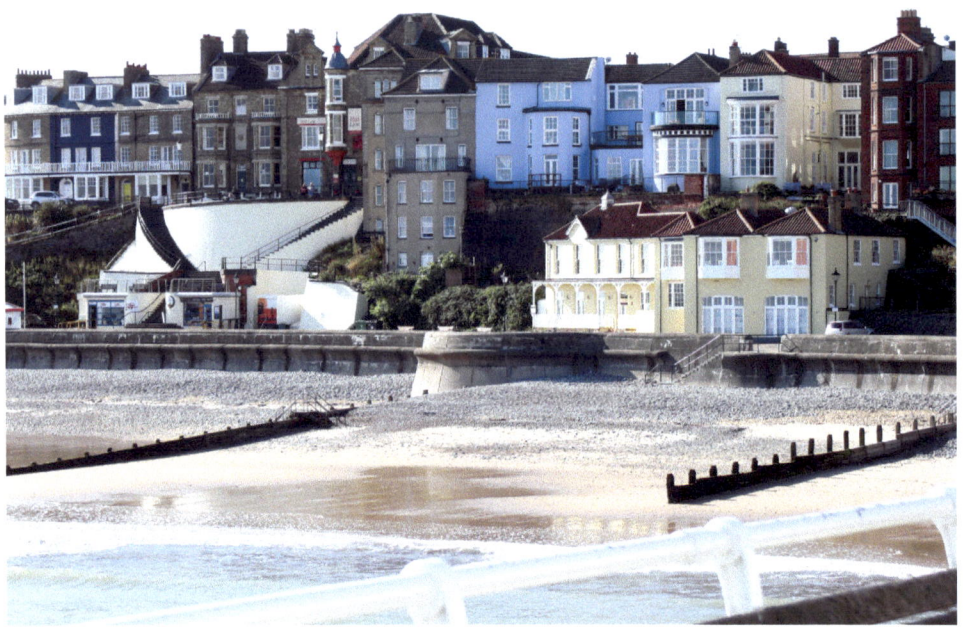

The Bath House in Cromer was an early day spa.

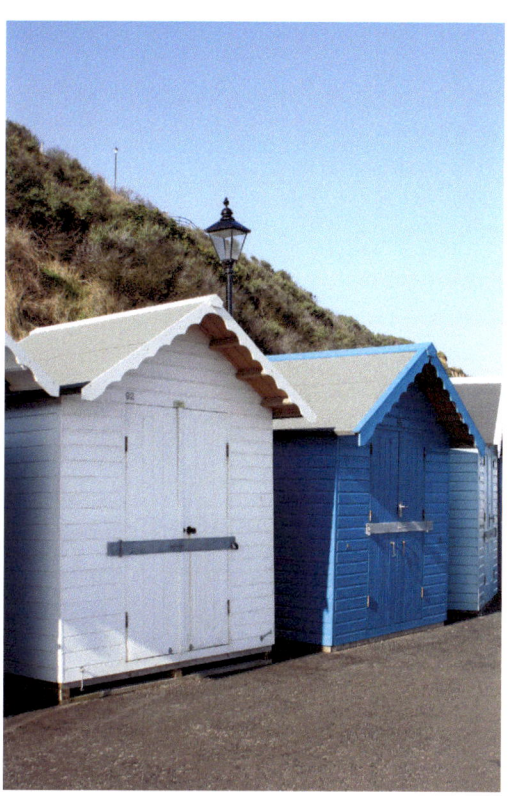

Crimean War ambulances were used for the
first beach huts.

therefore seemed a logical step to say that being exposed to the sun was healthy. Sunshine would be used to improve a range of health problems like skin ulcers, rickets and depression. Outdoor pursuits like cycling and tennis, and the suntanned glow associated with them, became popular, and for the middle classes, a tan meant you had the money to afford time at leisure. When Coco Chanel, a fashion idol of the 1920s, got sunburned by accident but flaunted it as the next fashion accessory, it was the final endorsement and the desire to be tanned began. In Britain, the reliability of the sun is suspect, but Cromer and Sheringham still had many sun worshippers. They would brave the often chilly beaches whenever the sun appeared in an attempt to tan.

It is now known that exposure to ultra violet rays in the sun is dangerous and that everyone needs to apply sun cream if their skin is exposed. The sun needs to be protected against, just as bathers enjoying the sea need to be protected from the dangers of the water.

As towns on the edge of the sea, the population of Cromer and Sheringham have always needed protection from the dangers associated with their location. Ships and boats have sought to navigate the shoreline safely throughout the history of both towns, and the earliest navigation aids were beacon fires or lamps. These were lit high on the cliffs, creating a light that could be seen out to sea and acting as a warning to shipping that they were close to land. During the fifteenth and sixteenth centuries the church tower of St Peter and St Paul in Cromer would display lamps to help show shipping where they

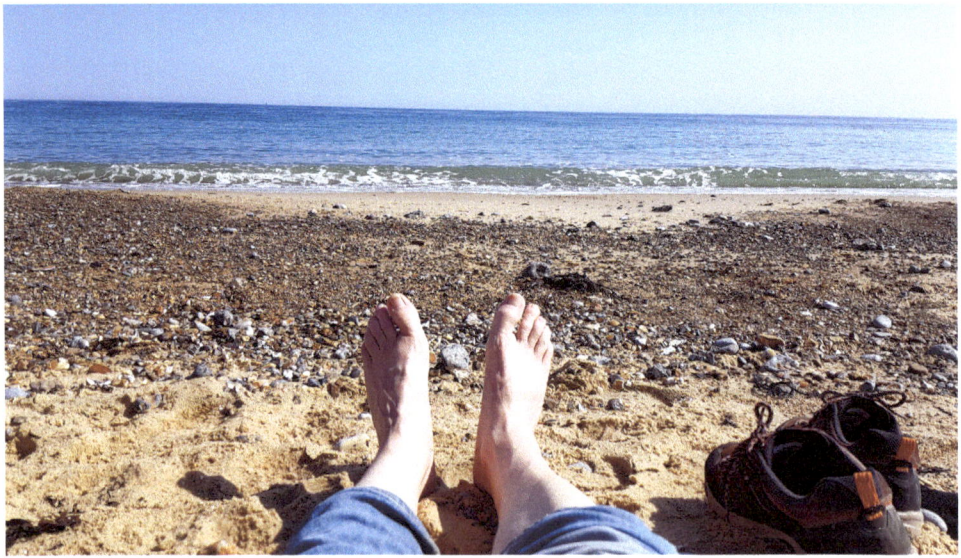

Relaxing on the beach and enjoying the sun.

were. This offered some protection for mariners but improvements were needed. The lights were often too dim to be seen through mist and vessels would come too close to shore before the warning was sounded.

DID YOU KNOW?
Edward Bach, the homeopath who developed Bach Flower Remedies, spent winters in Cromer in the 1930s. He enjoyed the healthy sea air and investigated local plants for their health-giving properties. Dr Bach believed he could connect with plants. When he felt a pain or negative emotion he would hold his hand over various flowers until the feeling passed. That plant was then attributed with the ability to cure. Most early Bach Flower Remedies were made in Cromer by collecting just the dew from plants. Dr Bach believed the plant's healing transferred through dew on its petals and he need not destroy the plant.

The first lighthouse was built in 1669 by John Clayton and George Blake. The lighthouse consisted of a flat-topped tower on which a coal beacon fire could be lit and kept burning. This privately run venture, although a means of giving aid to mariners, was also a money-making scheme. Clayton and Blake would charge any mariners who navigated by their lighthouse for the service, but few seafarers paid up, claiming they had not seen the light. Without income the owners could not afford to keep the beacon fires lit and the business soon failed.

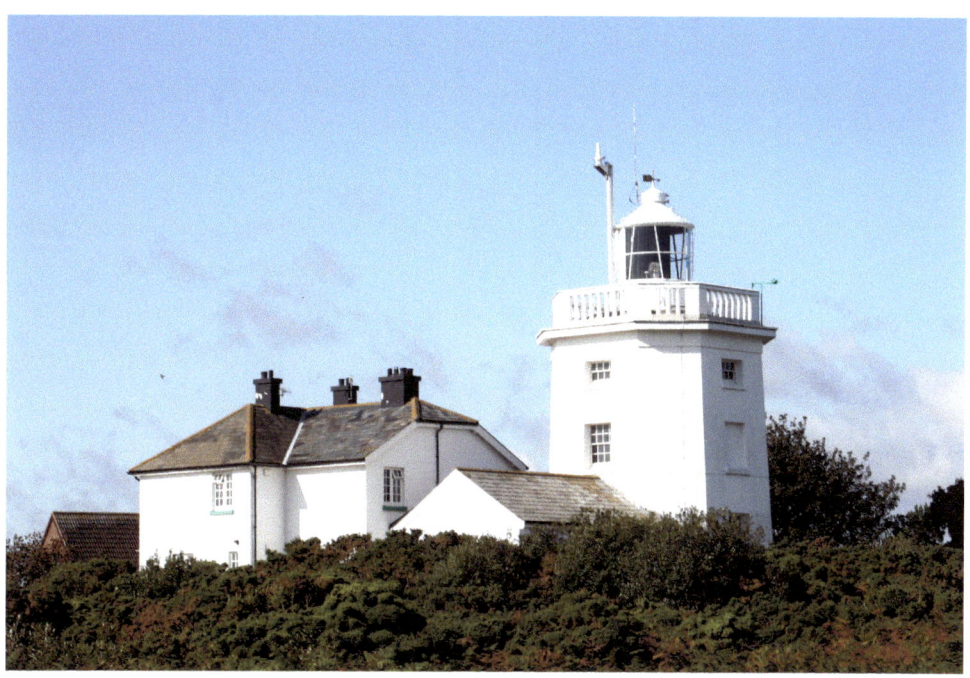

Cromer lighthouse has been in constant use since 1833.

The sea by the cliffs became treacherous without the light, and after only a few years out of service, the lighthouse was restored to use. It was taken over by Trinity House, a charitable organisation founded to help protect shipping and provide for aged mariners. The lighthouse building was kept in good repair and the light was constantly lit, but with the constant erosion by the sea, there was a danger of cliff falls. As the lighthouse crept ever closer to the cliff edge, the decision was made to build a new one further inland. The new lighthouse was completed in 1833 and stood half a mile from the cliff edge. It started to operate straight away, leaving the old one to the mercy of the waves, although it was to be another thirty years before the sea claimed the original tower.

During Victorian times the light was produced by an oil lamp and, to make it even more noticeable, rotating reflectors made the light appear to flash. Local fishermen had preferred the constant light and it took some time for them to accept the improvement. The lighthouse was finally electrified in the 1950s and it kept a lighthouse keeper until 1990 when it became automated. After three centuries, the lighthouse is still run by Trinity House under the name of the General Lighthouse Authority.

The Waterguard began in the early nineteenth century. The service was originally designated to be a deterrent to smuggling and had a chain of lookout stations around the coast. One of these still exists on Cromer seafront. The Old Lookout is now a privately owned property and the prominent upper window was used as one of the Waterguard's observation points in the nineteenth century, when the building was called Tucker's Hotel. Also in Cromer, on Cambridge Street, are terraced houses that were specially built to house the Waterguard officers. To prevent any relationships being formed between

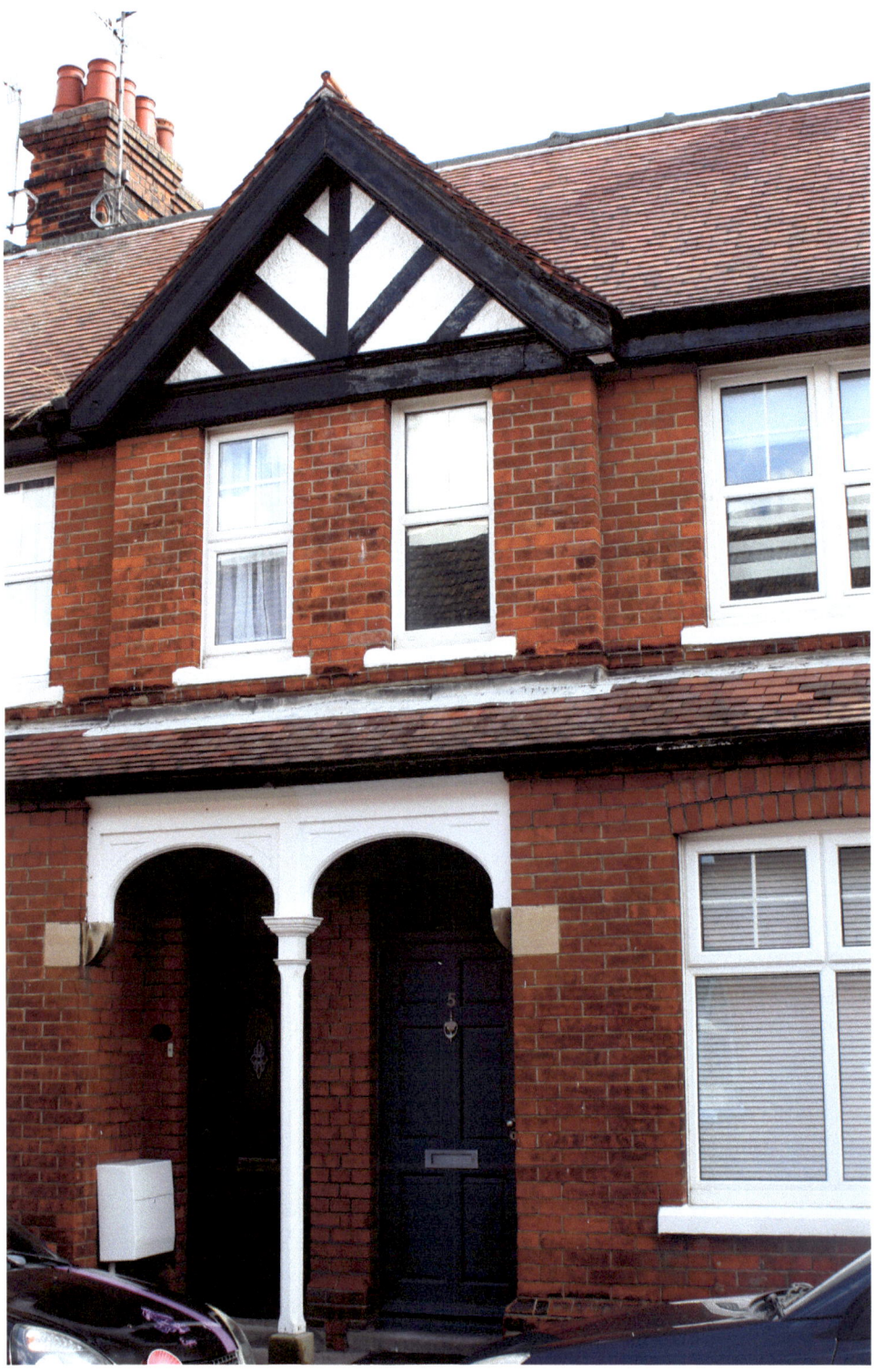

Victorian customs officers had their own accommodation to prevent dishonesty.

the officials and the locals, which may have led to the officers becoming less trustworthy, they were constantly moved around the different lookout stations and were boarded away from residents in Waterguard-controlled properties like these.

As smuggling decreased, the Waterguard was used as a lookout for ships in distress rather than for those contravening customs regulations. The Waterguard changed its name to the Coastguard and its role altered, becoming the service responsible for preserving the lives of those at sea and also the coordinator for the lifeboat service.

The Royal National Lifeboat Service has 237 lifeboat stations with 444 lifeboats and provides lifeguards on 200 beaches around Britain. It is a non-profit-making organisation and was founded in 1824. In its history, 600 lifeboatmen have been lost to the sea but they have saved 140,000 lives.

The Coastguard and the lifeboat services of Cromer and Sheringham need to be in constant contact with each other. This communication is vital to be able to alert the lifeboats of anyone in peril at sea. The telegraph system was the first means of communication used when the lifeboat service and Coastguard were first established. The principle of telegraph began during the Napoleonic Wars when chains of stations were set up along the coastline. The military would use semaphore to communicate what was happening at sea to the telegraph station, who would communicate it to the next,

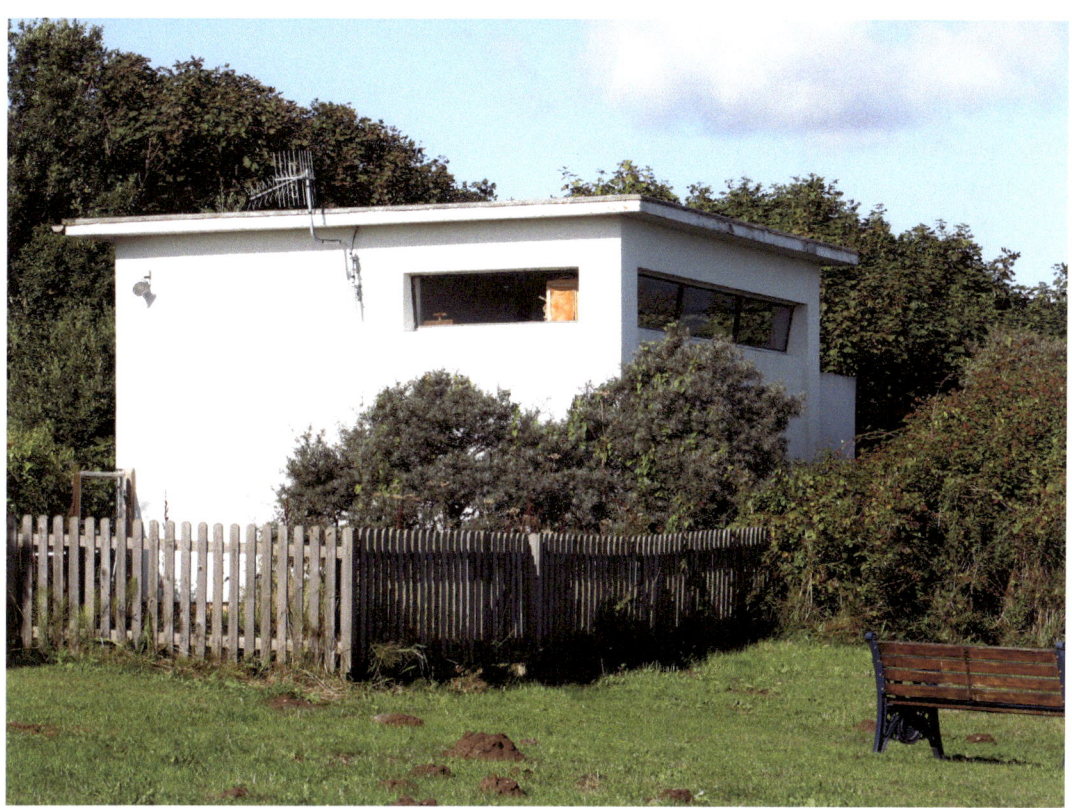

Now residential, this telegraph station was vital for sea rescue.

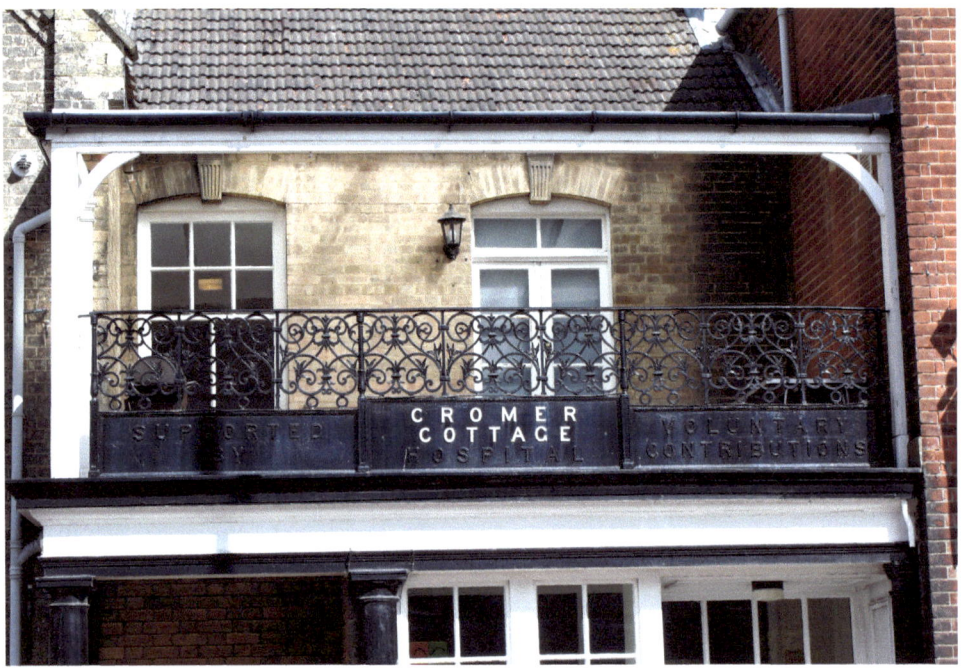

The Cottage Hospital had an early accident and emergency unit.

until the whole of the coast was systematically informed. This method was used until the invention of the electric telegraph in the 1850s, and in 1892 the Cromer and Sheringham lifeboats and the Coastguard were directly linked by telephone. From now on, both were instantly aware of anyone in difficulties and could quickly safeguard those near the sea.

Although Sheringham and Cromer are seaside towns, it isn't just those directly connected to the sea who need their health looking after. Up until the nineteenth century, most families dealt with medical matters by themselves using a common knowledge of herbal cures and remedies. If one person had slightly more knowledge of herbs and tinctures they would become known as the local healer and townsfolk would go to them to seek advice. The first doctors with some form of medical knowledge arrived in Cromer and Sheringham during the eighteenth century. They set up private practises to promote the health-giving properties of their water treatments but did not offer any sort of general medical advice. It was not until 1866 that proper medical provision was made for the area with the opening of the cottage hospital in Cromer.

The original hospital was created from two cottages and its six beds had to serve both Cromer and Sheringham for any cases of serious injury or illness. One extra bed was added twenty years later. Solely for use in the case of accident, it was a kind of forerunner to an accident and emergency bed. It became obvious that the hospital was not large enough and a new building was commissioned. Provided by Lord Suffield, it was built within the Suffield Park housing estate and, reflecting the style of the old cottage hospital, this too was built in a domestic style. The homely design also meant that it did not appear too clinical and institutional for its residential setting.

DID YOU KNOW?
The Bath House was originally built on Cromer Promenade in 1814. This house was washed away in a violent storm and rebuilt in 1836. Subsequent residents of the property have reported hearing unexplained noises on stormy nights. One Victorian resident said, 'It sounded like someone moving furniture around upstairs but I knew that I was alone.' It has been suggested since that the Bath House is haunted by the resident of the 1814 building, lost to the sea. On stormy nights, they can be heard desperately trying to save their belongings, and maybe themselves, from the devastating wind and waves.

Cromer hospital got its first X-ray machine in 1914 but before that, a Cromer resident had been the recipient of the first X-ray ever to be taken in Britain. In 1895, Lawrence Reynolds was shot in the head with a revolver in a hunting accident. He was taken to Cromer hospital, where the bullet was removed from his skull and his injuries treated. Mr Reynolds went on to live a normal life and suffered no after effects at all. However, the doctor who had treated him in Cromer hospital was so fascinated by the fact that Mr Reynolds had not died instantly or suffered any brain damage that he arranged for X-ray equipment to be sent from Germany. The doctor wanted to track the route the bullet had made through Mr Reynold's skull, and had heard about the new X-ray principle that

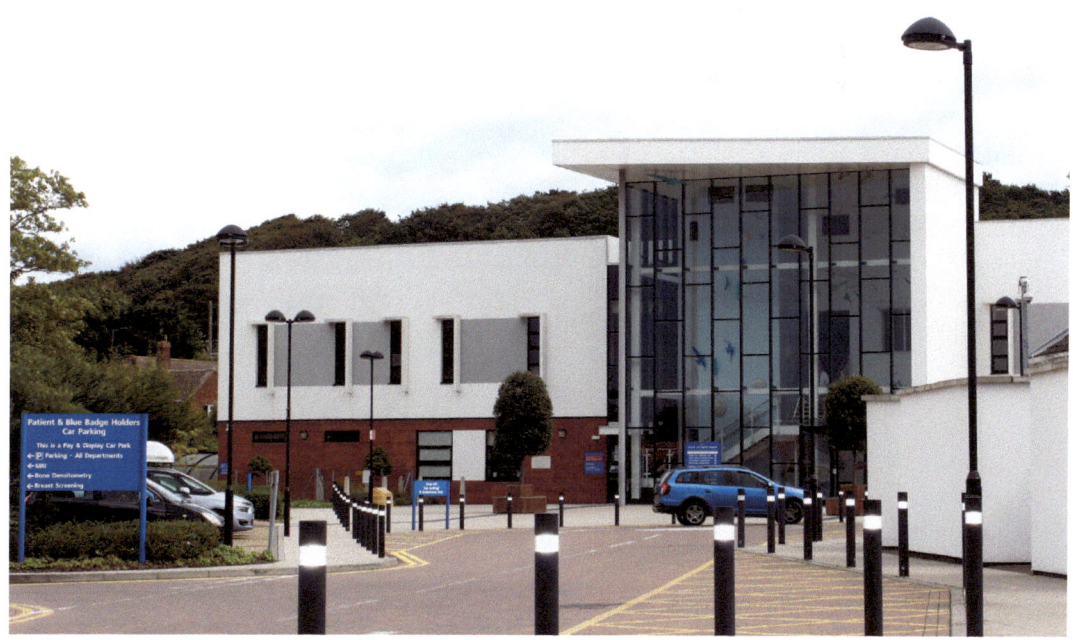

Modern additions to Cromer hospital complement its subtle 1930s style.

had only been discovered by Wilhelm Rontgen in that same year. Although X-rays were still in their infancy, the image of Lawrence Reynolds skull was successfully made, his doctor was able to study the results and this revealed that sheer luck had caused the bullet to miss Mr Reynolds brain by a fraction of an inch.

During the First World War and the Second World War both Sheringham and Cromer were the sites of convalescent military hospitals. When a serviceman was injured fighting overseas he was taken to the nearest military hospital for immediate care. When he had been successfully treated and was recovering, the soldier was taken back to Britain and to a convalescent hospital, where he would have time to fully regain his strength before being sent back to fight. In Cromer, Colne House Hotel was adapted for convalescence, as was The Dales Hotel in Sheringham. The Red House, a private residence, was turned into a fifty-bed hospital at the voluntary expense of the owners who wanted to help provide for the servicemen in every way they could.

Keeping everyone safe from danger with health and safety procedures is a major part of modern life. All of the emergency services in Cromer and Sheringham work tirelessly to keep residents, holidaymakers and visitors safe, even if it means putting themselves at risk. With a local environment ruled by nature and the sea, the vital work of the police, fire crew, ambulance service and lifeboats in the area goes quietly and determinedly on.

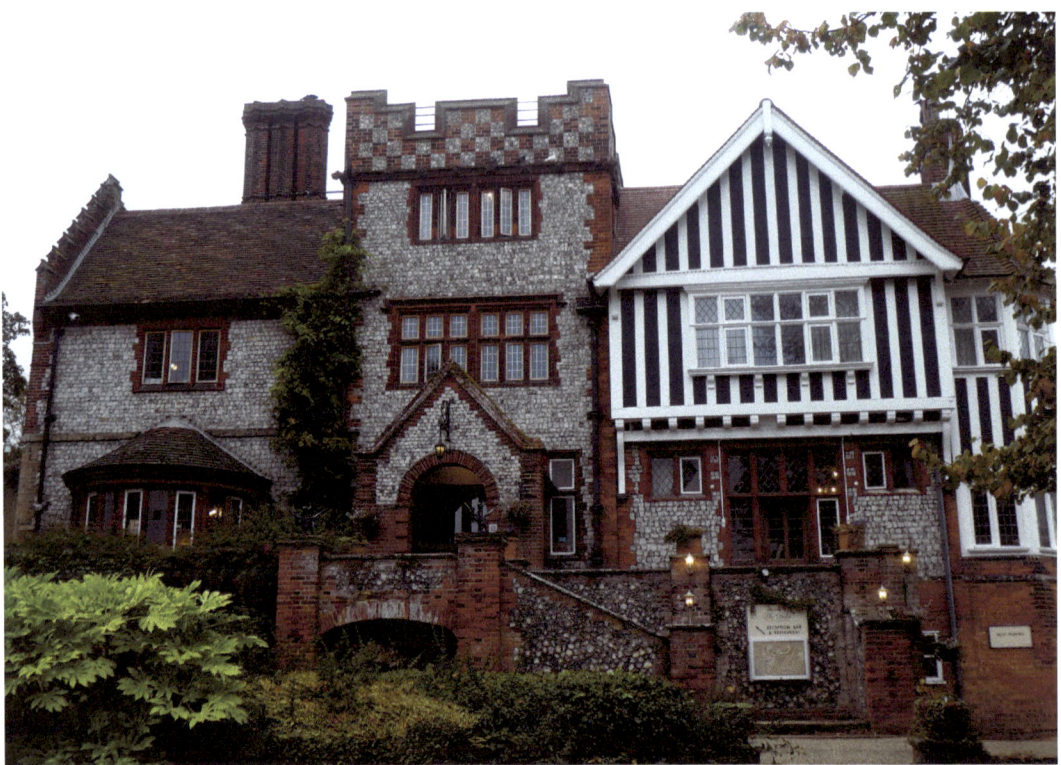

Hotels became convalescent hospitals for those injured in fighting overseas.

8. The Unsung Lifeboat Heroes

Lifeboats are an integral part of living in Cromer and Sheringham. Residents and visitors alike give the service all the support they can and there are regular lifeboat days to promote the Royal National Lifeboat Institution. These special events attract many tourists and the RNLI shops are regularly visited by shoppers on the high streets. These both add much needed funds to the charity. Both lifeboat stations are often open to the public, and yet there is a lot about the history of the RNLI, its involvement in saving lives at Cromer and Sheringham, and the accomplishments of both its boats and its men that isn't widely known.

The sea around the Cromer and Sheringham coast is notorious for sandbanks, and vessels trying to navigate them have always been at risk of getting into distress, especially in the frequent bad weather. From the earliest times the townspeople have had a willingness to go out and assist mariners in trouble, but before the lifeboat service arrived this was just in their small fishing boats. Despite the seamanship of the Cromer and Sheringham fishermen, their small boats were often at the mercy of the waves more than the vessel in distress and many lives were lost.

In 1785 the first prototype lifeboat was produced. Lionel Lukin developed a boat designed to stay upright and stable regardless of the roughness of the sea. This was achieved by adding a second keel to add weight below the waterline, and incorporating air-filled bulkheads and cork buoyancy aids above the waterline. The first lifeboat was used at Bamburgh in Northumberland, but many more were built and they soon became invaluable to the communities around the coastline of Great Britain. The Royal National Lifeboat institution (or RNLI) was founded in 1824 and used the Lukin-designed lifeboats to provide a nationwide service to save lives at sea.

The first lifeboat and lifeboat house in Sheringham, however, was a private donation by the Upcher family in 1838. Local boatbuilders were used to build the lifeboat the *Augusta*, which went on to save around a thousand lives. The service was privately funded until the RNLI took over the running of the lifeboat station in 1867. A new lifeboat station was built, although it soon needed replacing by a larger one, which was built at the end of the Esplanade. This one is still used by the modern service. Sheringham has had just eleven lifeboats in its two-century history with the RNLI. There is great pride in the boats and Sheringham is the only town to still have any of their original lifeboats. Four are on display in Sheringham museum.

Cromer lifeboat station has been at the end of the pier since 1923. This location, however, means it is the most exposed lifeboat station in the country and suffers badly from the effects of the weather. As the weather had taken its toll, a new lifeboat house was built in 1999, and the original station was taken to Southwold in Suffolk where, aptly, it has become a lifeboat museum.

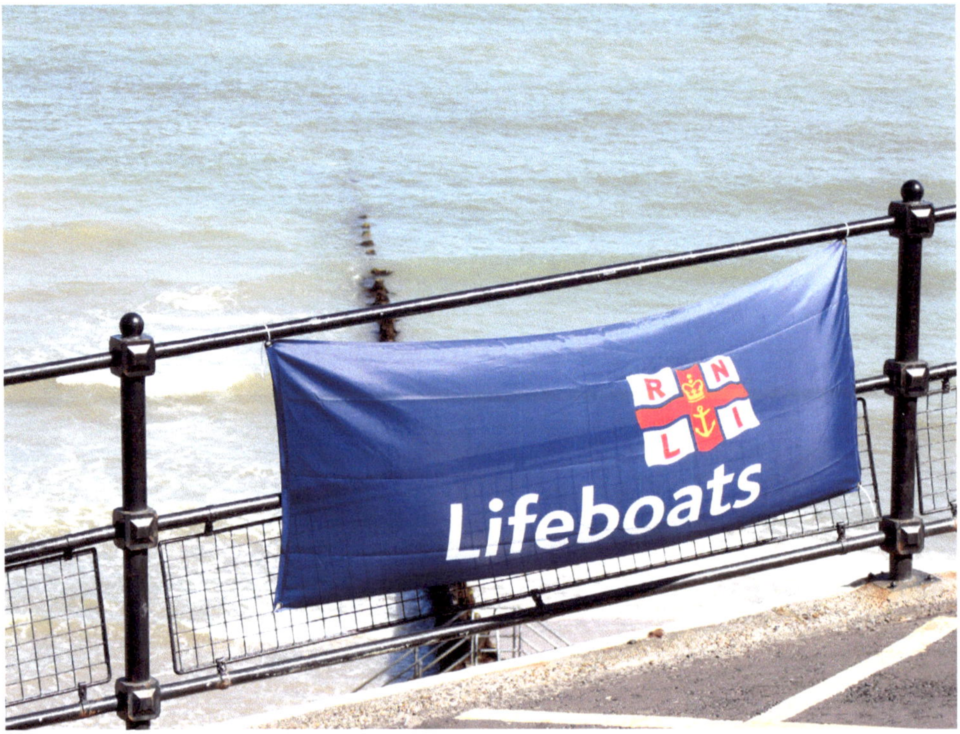

The Royal National Lifeboat Institution protects thousands of lives.

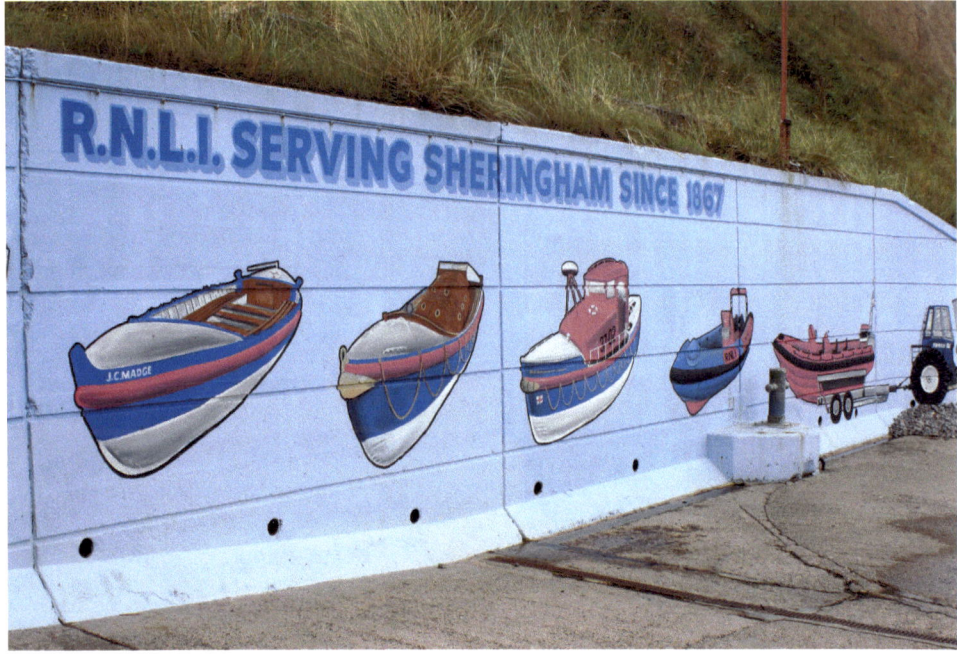

Lifeboat design has changed little in 200 years.

The lifeboat service in Cromer also started as a private enterprise but lack of funding meant it soon hit financial problems. The condition of the lifeboat deteriorated so much that it was no longer seaworthy and could not be used as a means of rescue. The lifeboat station was taken over by the RNLI in 1857 but they still struggled to keep the lifeboat seaworthy. Benjamin Bond Cabbell, a politician who had a summer home in Cromer, donated a new lifeboat and lifeboat station to the town in 1868, which resulted in Cromer finally having a proper, safe lifeboat service. An additional lifeboat, a motorised one, was purchased in 1923 and this prompted the construction of the lifeboat house on the end of the pier. The pier-end location made launching the new boat easier and safer. The boat could be launched even at low tide and it was beyond any groynes or rocks that could damage the propeller.

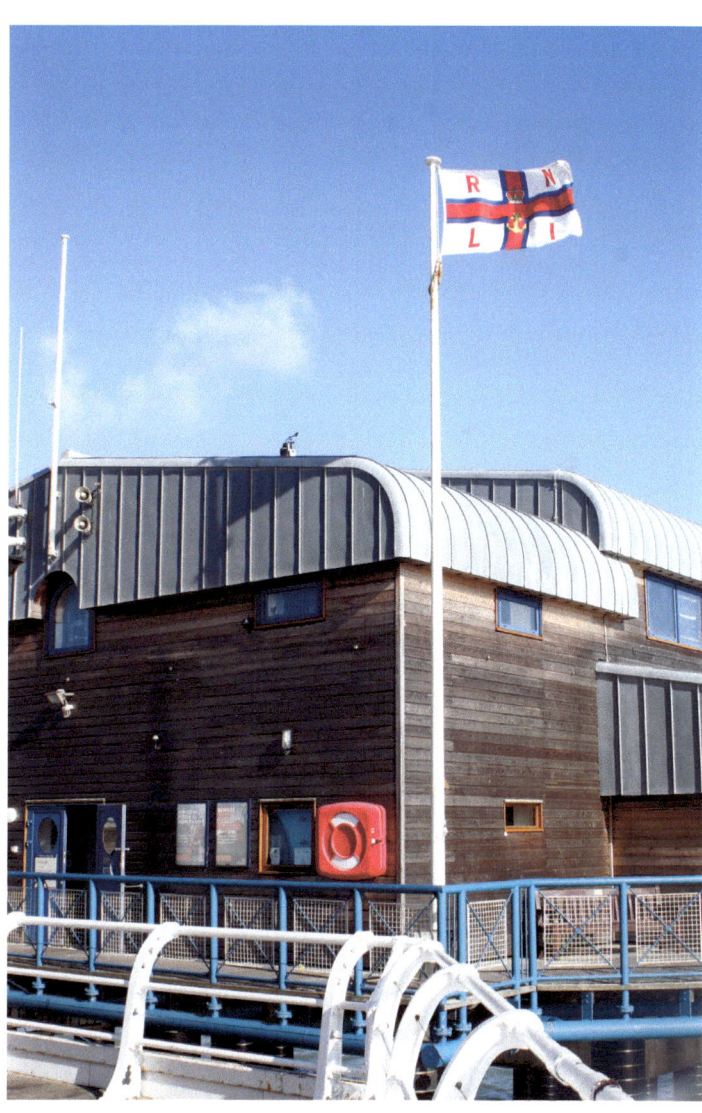

Cromer's lifeboat station is at the mercy of the waves.

DID YOU KNOW?
The *Augusta* was Sheringham's first lifeboat. Donated by the Upcher family in memory their daughter and named for her, the boat was a sixteen-oar vessel and saved many lives. The boat was eventually deemed no longer seaworthy and sold on. In the 1950s, The *Augusta* was rediscovered in the Norfolk Broads, where she had been cut in half and used to shelter small pleasure boats. Such is the affection of the Sheringham residents for its lifeboats that some of the *Augusta*'s hull was purchased by a local businessman and he had the wooden planking preserved in saltwater tanks.

Cromer lifeboat station sits between two major and potentially lethal sandbanks, the Sheringham Shoal and Haisborough Sands, and frequent bad weather conditions create frequent call-outs. However, despite the indispensable nature of the lifeboats it did not stop the trained crewmen getting their call-up papers during the Second World War. The coxswain at the time questioned the validity of the call-up, pointing out that while his men may be volunteers, they should be considered as being in a reserved occupation due to the importance of their work, and be exempt from serving overseas. The response from the Home Office was that the crew were needed in the forces and there were many other men in Cromer who were capable of manning the lifeboats. It was true that there were many skilled seamen still resident in Cromer, but this was due to their age. The volunteer lifeboat crew for the rest of the war, therefore, were mainly septuagenarians.

The coxswain during the Second World War, who fought to keep his trained crew with him, was the most famous lifeboat coxswain the country has ever known, Henry Blogg. Over a fifty-three-year career he was responsible for saving 873 lives in 387 callouts. He was awarded the George Cross and the British Empire Medal, which makes him the most decorated member of any lifeboat team in the country. Unlike most other Cromer and Sheringham fishermen Henry Blogg was only ever known by his given name, never a nickname. This quiet and dogged man was unique. Henry's nephew described him as, 'Never one to give in, if my uncle started a job he would have to continue until he had finished it, he was one of a kind.'

Henry Blogg had simple beginnings. His mother, Ellen, was unmarried when he was born in 1873 but she later married into the Davies family. Her husband, James, was coxswain of Cromer lifeboat at the time of their marriage and Henry joined him in the service when he was eighteen years old. In 1901 Henry married Annie Brackenbury and they went on to have two children, a son and a daughter, who sadly both died young. When his stepfather retired in 1909 it was Henry who had proved himself to be the most suitable successor and he took over the role of the Cromer lifeboat coxswain. Away from his voluntary work with the RNLI, Henry Blogg was an excellent crab fisherman and also ran a family business hiring out beach huts and deckchairs.

Manning the lifeboats was a physically challenging role. The boats were all rowboats during Henry's time as coxswain, and had to be manually launched deep into the waves

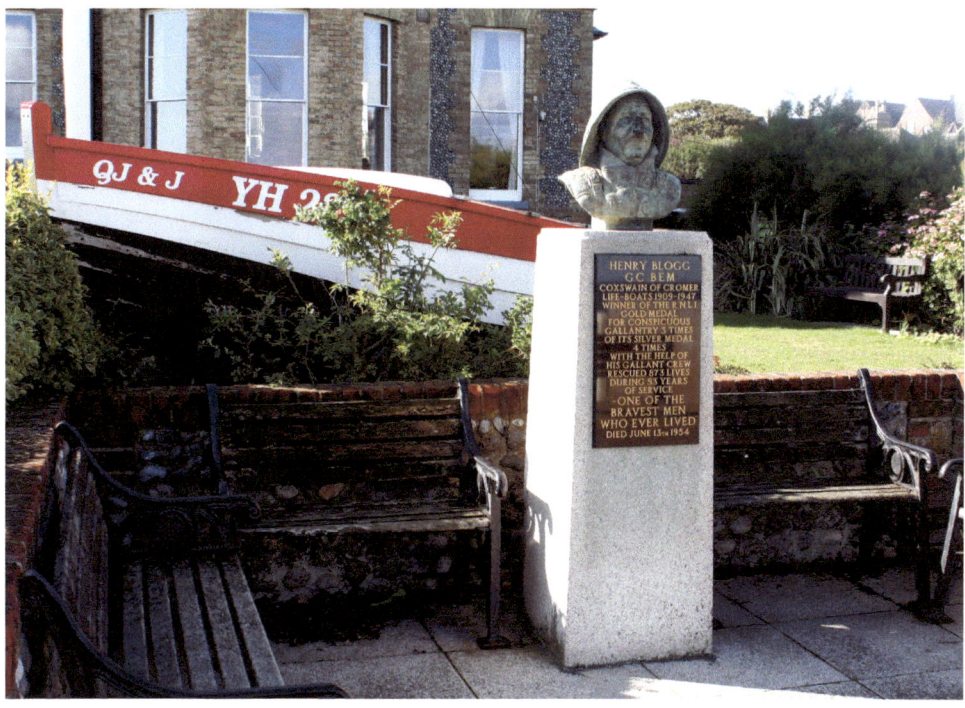

The memorial to Henry Blogg looks over his beloved sea.

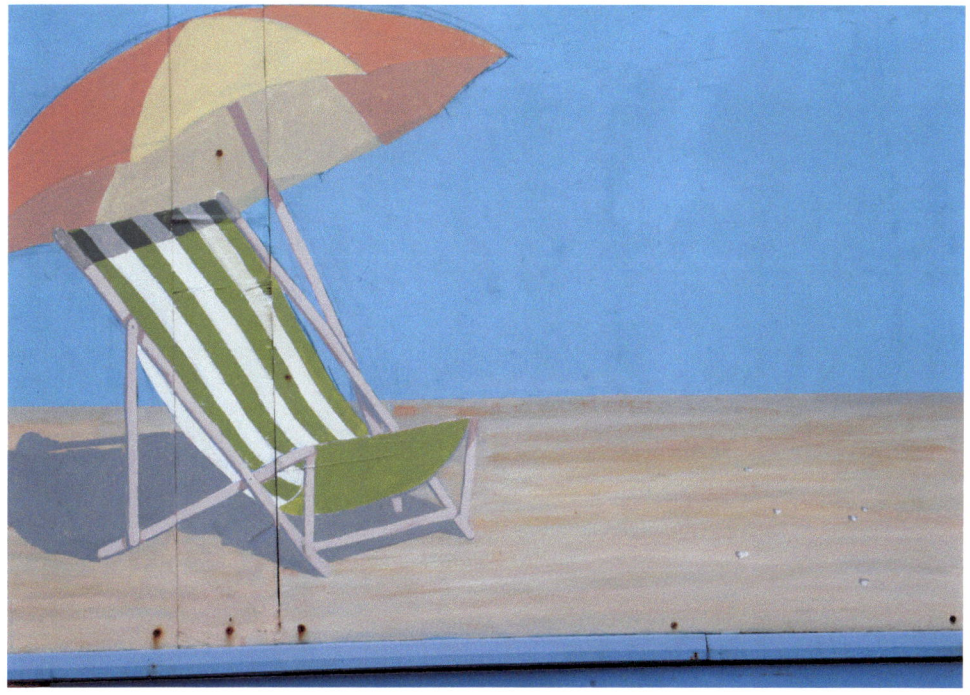

Wall art in Sheringham portrays Henry Blogg's family business.

from an open beach. If the launch was not deep enough, the power of the waves would propel the lifeboat back onto shore and the tiring task would have to begin again. One lifeboat rescue that brought medals for the crew challenged them to the point of exhaustion. In 1917 the lifeboat was called out to aid the steamship *The Pyrin*, which had got into difficulties some miles out from Cromer. The lifeboat crew rowed out to the far point on the horizon where *The Pyrin* was in trouble, picked up the crew of the stricken vessel, and started to row back. While this was happening another ship, *The Fernebo*, hit a mine and was broken in half. Some of the men from this Swedish ship managed to get to their own life raft. Henry Blogg and his men safely got the crew of *The Pyrin* back to shore just as a dinghy from one half of *The Fernebo* attempted to land at Cromer. The lifeboat was safely landed but the dinghy from *The Fernebo* overturned in the rough breakers near the beach. The lifeboatmen waded out into the rough sea and pulled each sailor safely ashore. It then became apparent that the crew from the other half of *The Fernebo* were still stranded out in the North Sea. Henry and his team tried to launch the lifeboat for a second mission but the rolling breakers forced the boat back on to the beach. The crew tried again, and again, and finally, after many exhausting attempts, the lifeboat was launched and the long row out to *The Fernebo* started. There followed a successful rescue of the remaining crew but by the time Henry and his crew returned to the lifeboat station nearly twenty-four hours had passed since they had first rowed out to *The Pyrin*. They had spent an entire day at sea aiding others.

Another example of Henry Blogg's doggedness came about in 1941 when the SS *English Trader* ran aground. The Cromer lifeboat rowed out to assist the crew of the stranded

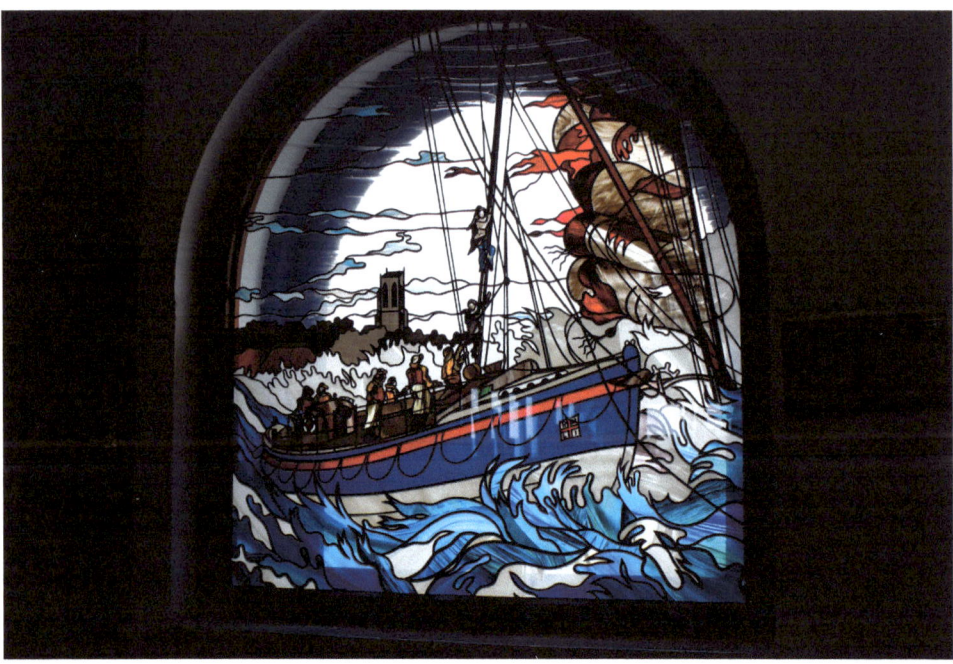

There were gruelling twenty-four-hour rescues out of Cromer.

vessel, but just as they were approaching the ship enormous waves partly capsized the lifeboat. Henry and another four of his crew were lost overboard. Henry was an excellent seaman and yet he never learned to swim. The second in command took control of the lifeboat, stabilised it and went back to pick up each member of the lifeboat crew from the appalling seas. One of the rescued crew, Walter Allen, suffered heart failure so Henry took the decision to row to Great Yarmouth, the nearest port to them, to get him medical help. After doing this, the coxswain and crew rowed back to Cromer to renew the attempt to rescue those on board the *English Trader*. The Cromer lifeboat picked up every one of the crew and brought them safely to land at Cromer. Sadly, Walter Allen later died in hospital.

In 1947 Henry Blogg retired as coxswain but would still watch every launch of the lifeboat from a vantage point on the promenade. Four years after his retirement, Henry Blogg died. He is remembered with great affection and respect and has a museum dedicated to him, run by the RNLI.

Henry's successor as coxswain was Henry Davies, his nephew, who was always known as 'Shrimp'. Henry Blogg himself had coined the nickname, when he saw how tiny his nephew was as a newborn baby. Shrimp was born in 1914 and, like his uncle before him, joined the lifeboat volunteers at eighteen years of age. Shrimp Davies went on over 500 rescues in his twenty-nine-year career as coxswain. The day before he retired in 1976, Shrimp was made the subject of the TV show *This Is Your Life* and was surprised by Eammon Andrews and the big red book at the end of Cromer pier. Between retiring from

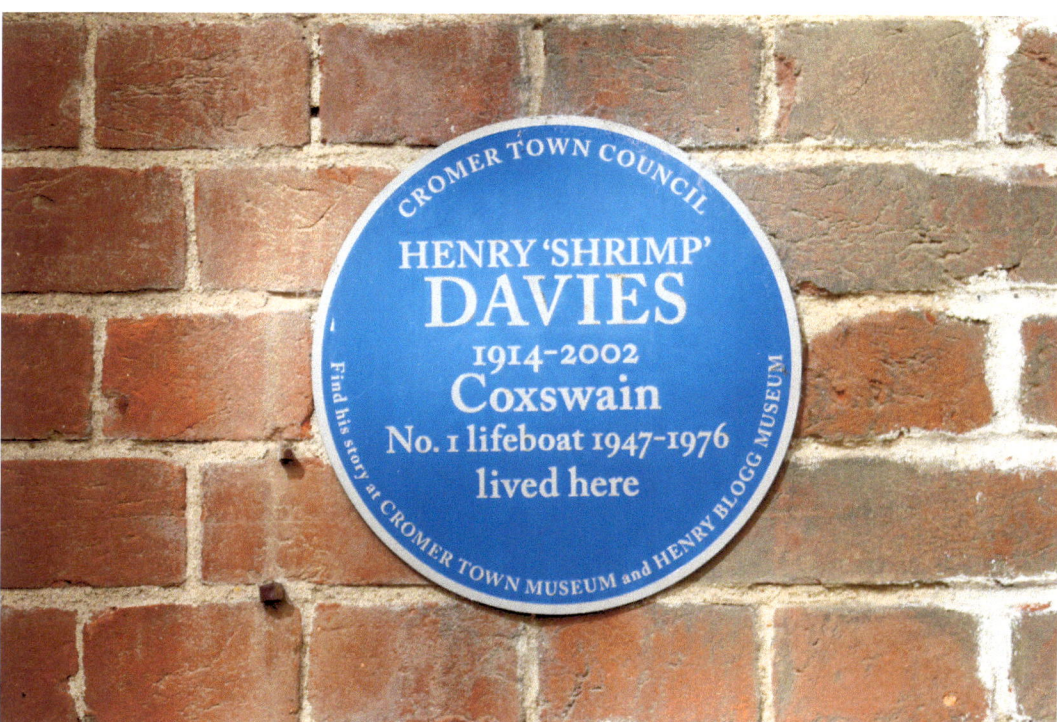

Henry 'Shrimp' Davies lived in Cromer all of his life.

the service and his death in 2002, Shrimp continued to run the family business, hiring out deckchairs. Six generations of the Davies family have been in continuous service as lifeboatmen in Cromer.

The lifeboats kept at Cromer and Sheringham lifeboat stations have become nearly as famous as their heroic coxswains. In Cromer, the lifeboat *HF Bailey*, under the command of Henry Blogg, served the station from 1935 to 1945. The boat was called out 134 times in her ten years of service and saved the lives of 514 seamen. The most lives saved by this lifeboat at one time was 111 from the trader SS *Meriones* in January 1941. The SS *Meriones* had become stranded on the notorious Haisborough Sands in bad weather, and before the crew could be rescued, the merchant ship came under attack from enemy aircraft. The *HF Bailey* arrived just as anti-aircraft gunfire from a nearby British naval ship had overwhelmed the enemy bombers and driven them off. The 111-strong crew were all saved by the Cromer lifeboat crew before the bombers returned and left the SS *Meriones* as a wreck on the sea bed.

In Sheringham, their lifeboat *Foresters Centenary* served between 1936 and 1961. During the Second World War, Sheringham was below the flight path to many RAF bases further inland. The lifeboat was often called out to aircraft that had ditched into the sea on their return flight due to damage obtained on their mission. Of the fifty-six times during the war that *Foresters Centenary* was called out, thirty-four of those occasions were to ditched aircraft. This led to the lifeboat being affectionately known as the 'Airmen's Lifeboat' by the many servicemen who owed their lives to both it and the *Foresters Centenary* crew.

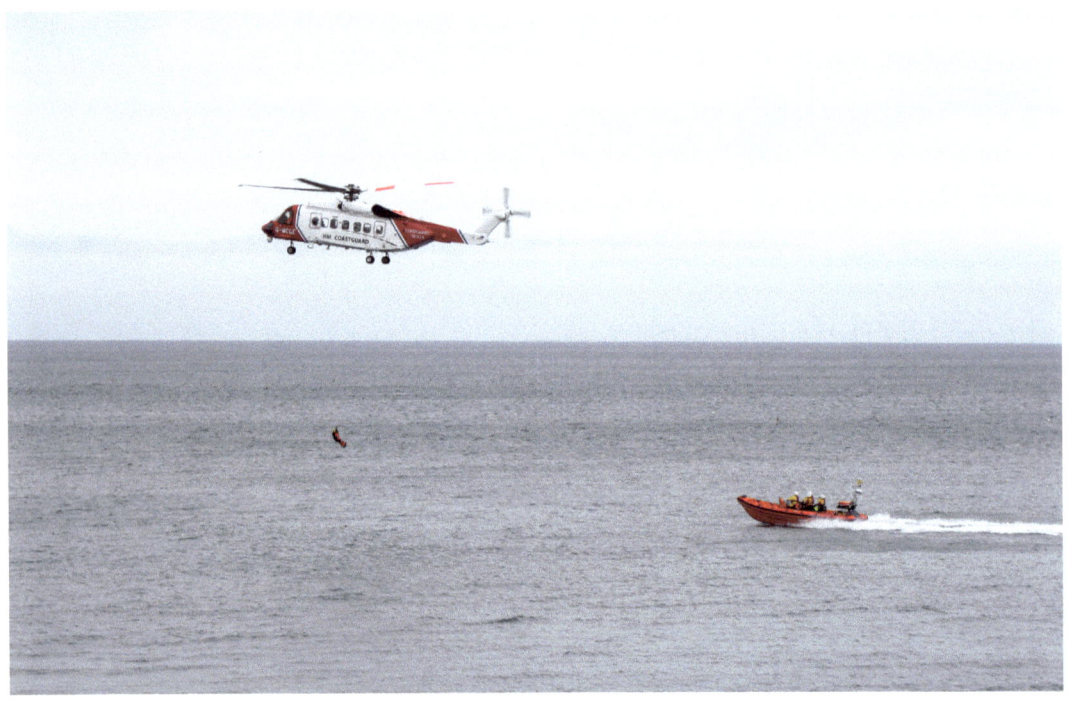

The modern lifeboat service has a variety of equipment available.

DID YOU KNOW?
The term coxswain is the official title for the head of a lifeboat crew. Although the most important person in the lifeboat station and the senior crew member, the name coxswain literally means 'boat servant'. It derivates from both the Anglo-Saxon word 'cockleboat', which was a small dinghy towed behind a larger ship, and 'sveinn', which was the old Norse word for servant. Humble beginnings for what has become such a crucial lifesaving role.

In contrast to the occasions when hundreds of lives are saved are those times that are quiet for the lifeboat service. The Cromer and Sheringham lifeboats may only be called out a handful of times in a season and, thankfully, on none of those occasions will there be any danger to life. Some of the lifeboat's call-outs turn out to be false alarms. The lifeboat and crew have been called on to investigate objects at sea that have been seen by the general public and mistaken for someone in distress. For example, a black plastic sack that had become partly filled with air was mistaken for an upturned boat and a swimmer reported for being too far out to sea turned out to be a very healthy dog. When the lifeboat approached the dog, who was enjoying the waves, it swam nonchalantly past the crew and returned safely to shore while the lifeboatmen looked on in relieved amusement.

Any time the lifeboats are called out it is an act of bravery on their part. The volunteer lifeboat crew are always there, ready to risk their own lives to save others in danger.

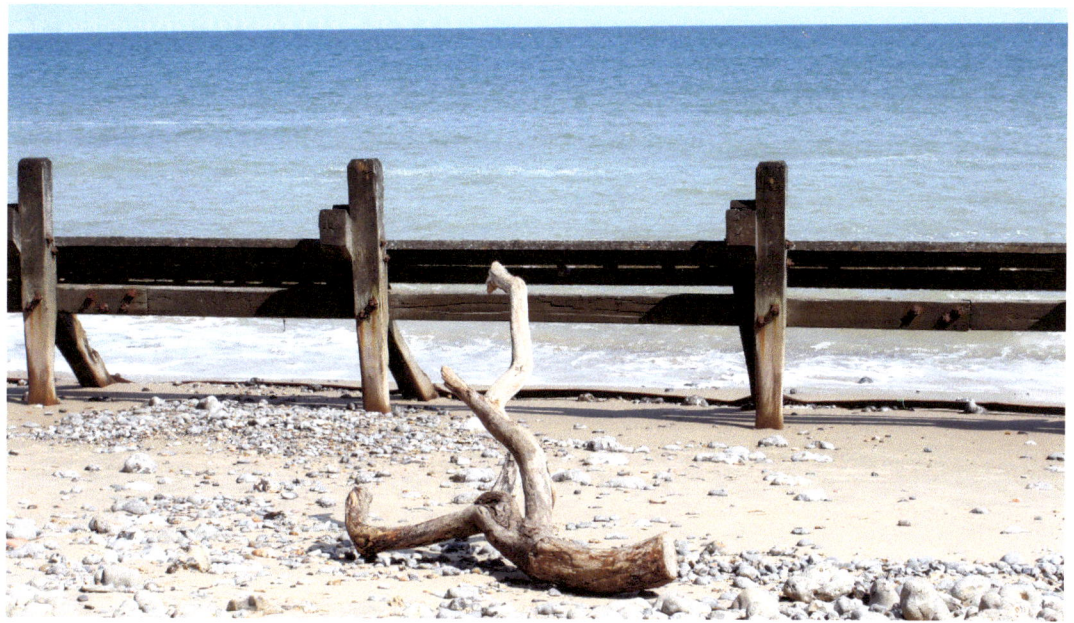

Lifeboats are always on alert, even with a calm sea.

9. The Secrets Behind Café Culture

Cafés, coffee shops and tearooms are a major focal point on the seafronts and down the main streets in Cromer and Sheringham. A visit to either town would not be the same without taking time out to sit, have a hot drink and watch the world go by. Trends change and while the almost clinical coffee shops of today replace some of the 'greasy spoons' of fifty years ago or the temperance houses that were around a century and a half ago, the ethos remains the same. To relax at the seaside means to relax over a cuppa. The historical facts of this typically British tradition are fascinating to discover.

Tea drinking gained popularity and status during the seventeenth and eighteenth centuries. Claims that tea remedied all kinds of ailments, its exclusivity due to expense, and the fact that it was drunk by the royal family meant that it became fashionable for the rich to drink tea in the exclusive coffee houses of London. When the high tax duty on the import of tea was relaxed, it became cheaper to import and buy tea and therefore more widely available to everyone. It was no longer just for the very wealthy.

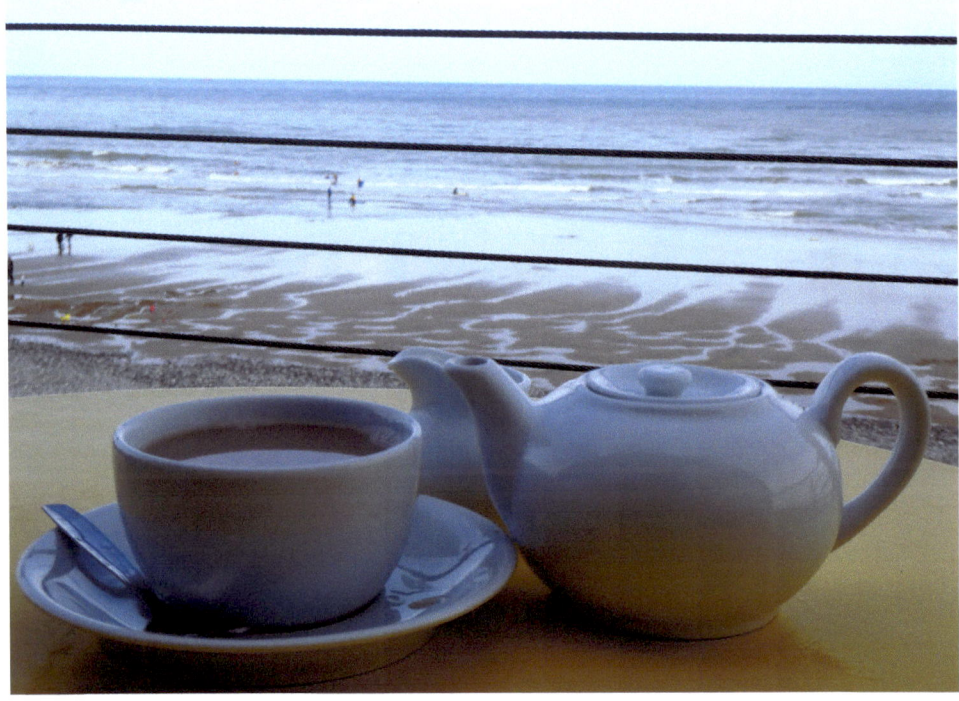

A hot cuppa will keep out the chilly sea breeze.

As tea was said to be good for the health, and seaside towns like Cromer and Sheringham were destinations to go to improve general well-being, it was a natural step that establishments in the resorts started to serve tea. The first tea lounge in Cromer opened in 1817 and formed part of The Wellington Hotel. The whole of the upper floor was put aside for tea drinking and it became a very fashionable place to be seen in. Other inns and hotels followed suit and soon most hostelries in Sheringham and Cromer were serving tea alongside ale and beer.

By the 1880s, as drinking tea had become customary for the British population, so there was a growing trend towards the prohibition of alcohol. The Temperance Society had begun. It was started by wealthy residents of many large towns and cities who did not approve of the drunkenness they had witnessed by the working classes. They tried (unsuccessfully) to prevent this behaviour by getting alcohol prohibited. In addition, the society tried to discourage people from drinking alcohol by offering an alternative, unlicensed venue. They started to open establishments they advertised as 'somewhere working men can drink tea and coffee at a reasonable price and get social and intellectual recreation.' The Lord Nelson Coffee Tavern was opened by the Temperance Society in Cromer. It was an alcohol-free place for fishing families to enjoy themselves and relax. Although used by some, the idea of the temperance house did not catch on, but the pleasure derived from drinking tea and coffee in a relaxed social setting did. The desire to spend quality time in a tearoom or café started to creep into people's routines and when reasonably priced food was also offered, this heralded the culture of the traditional seaside 'caff' so loved by visitors to Cromer and Sheringham.

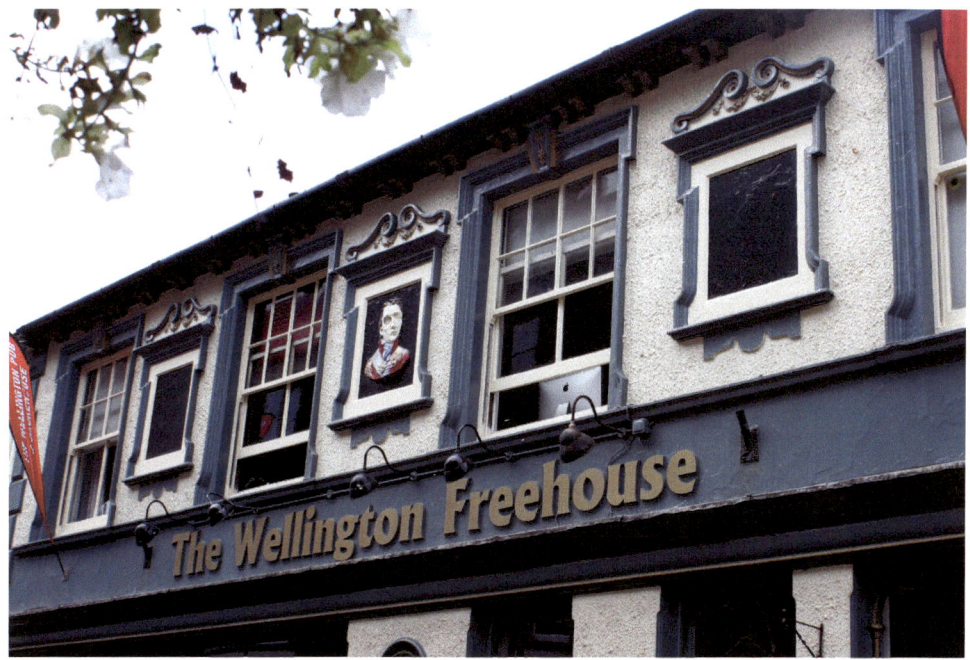

The Wellington had a fashionable Victorian tea lounge upstairs.

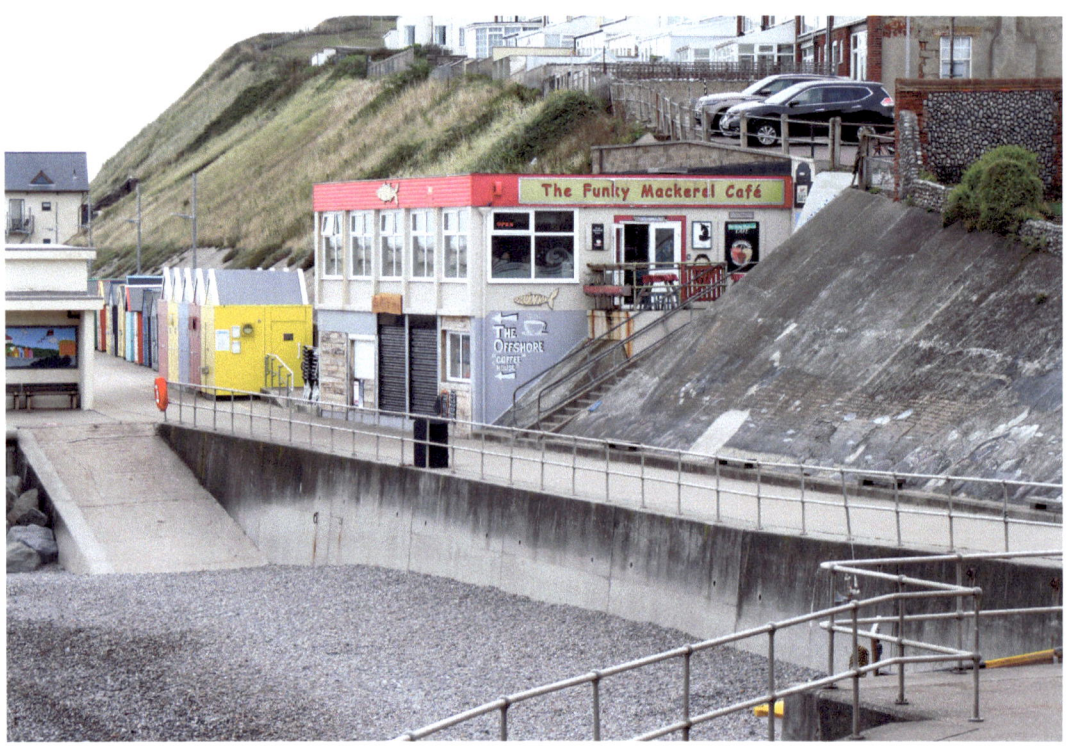

Traditional seaside cafés still provide traditional seaside fare.

The first café in Cromer was called Bay House and opened on Garden Street, offering tea, sandwiches and cakes. The property is still there and although at first glance the façade looks modern, the bay windows that gave the café its name remain. The inset doorway and knapped flint walls also reveal that the property dates back to the nineteenth century. A café still occupies the site continuing the 150-year history of offering refreshments for tourists.

Sheringham's oldest café is The Pretty Corner Tea Gardens. Originally occupying a wooden hut and serving an occasional walker, the café started in 1926 and has been on the same site ever since. The Tea Garden Cafe grew in size as the popularity of Pretty Corner grew and this picturesque establishment is now well loved by walkers and picnickers. When Pretty Corner first opened, attitudes about preserving the countryside were a lot different to modern ideals. A Sheringham guidebook, dating from the early twentieth century, includes this suggestion: 'Picnicking here is encouraged, but there is a worry from the estate owners that the debris (like papers and tins) from such activities be scattered to the winds. Such rubbish should be placed under stones to prevent this.' Hopefully this advice was not taken, the litter taken home and the beauty of the scene preserved for following visitors.

Tea shops themselves can be a picturesque sight to behold. The Sitting Room in Sheringham commands a lovely corner spot and looks over to where the open-air theatre, the Arcade Lawn, used to be. The red-brick building has an elegant bayed front and the

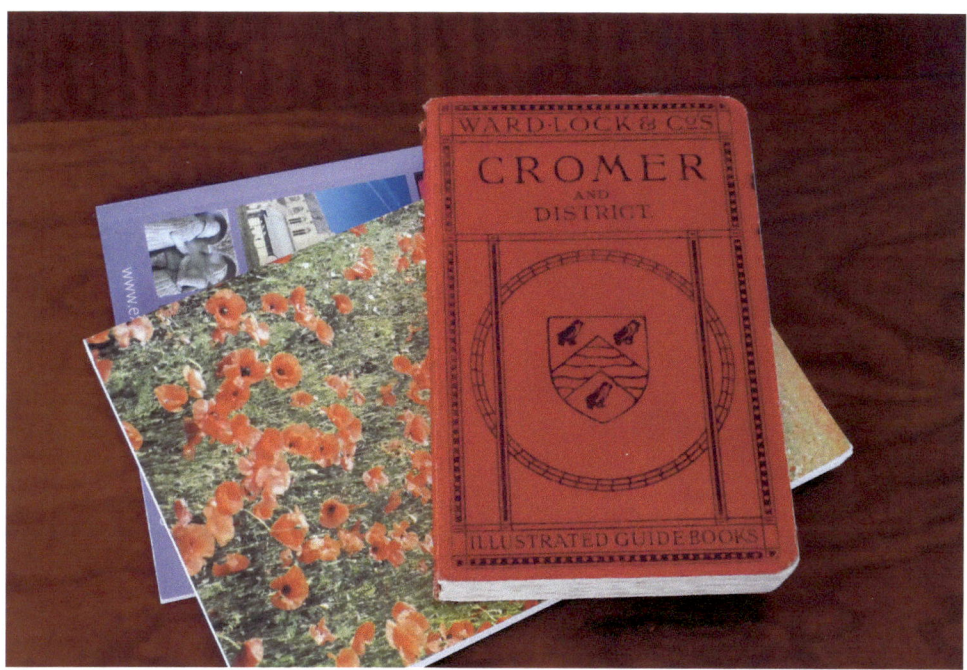

Old guidebooks can offer some rather curious advice.

outside seating area sits among Victorian shopfronts. A similarly lovely scene is provided by the Lifeboat Café in Cromer. It's long glazed front and seating terrace is as much a view to photograph as the old lifeboat station situated opposite, or the expanse of sea and beach that the café overlooks.

DID YOU KNOW?
The Funky Mackerel is a Sheringham café that commands a great view over the beach and out to the Sheringham Shoal wind farm. This view was once dominated by the departure or arrival of the fishing fleet, often in bad weather. The café used to be called Shannocks Café. Shannock is a colloquial term for the inhabitants of Sheringham and is reputed to mean 'wild and reckless people'. This is an apt term for those fishermen of the past who went out to sea in all weathers to provide for their families.

The esplanades of both Cromer and Sheringham have seafront complexes at the base of their sea walls that incorporate beach huts, kiosks and cafés. They date from a time between the First and Second World Wars, when a newly emerging group of young visitors started to arrive and wanted cafés and tearooms to reflect their modern, bright tastes. A short economic boom had followed the First World War and social restrictions for young women started to relax. This led to young, unmarried people having spending power and a desire to have fun and holiday in popular seaside resorts like Cromer and Sheringham. Their arrival produced the need for the new buildings. The impact of the sea and the weather mean these pieces of art deco architecture look a little faded now, but it is easy to imagine how vibrant and lively they were at the time.

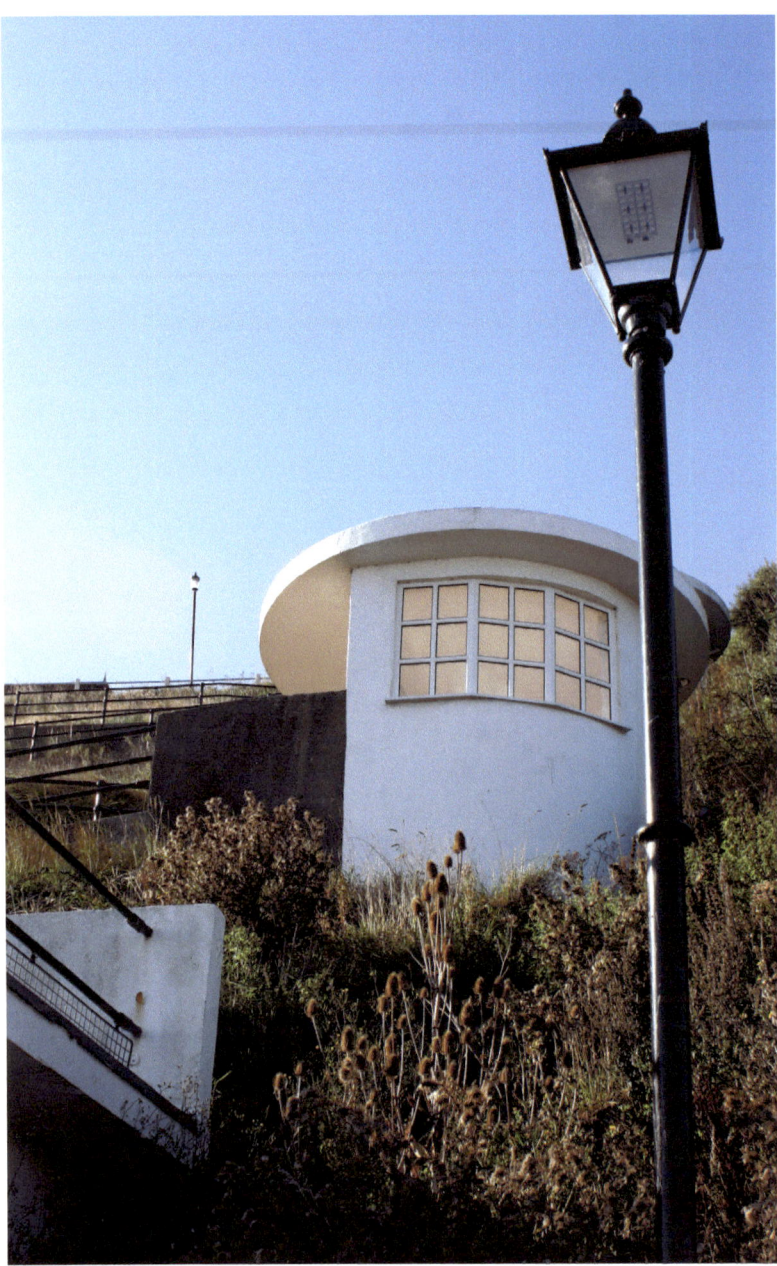

There is striking art deco architecture in Cromer and Sheringham.

Cafés, even after they have closed their doors for the last time, are fondly remembered. Opposite the Church of St Peter and St Paul, in Cromer, stood the Tudor Café. A private house was converted into the tearoom in the mid-twentieth century and it was clad in the mock-Tudor beams that are still painted black and white to this day. The café, which could seat a whole coach trip at one sitting, is remembered with affection. Cromer residents and visitors still call it the Tudor Café even though it ceased trading many years ago. In contrast, other premises that have changed to become cafés are remembered for the establishment they used to be. There was an elegant lingerie shop in Cromer, on the corner of Church Street and Overstrand Road. Elizabeth's is remembered for its wonderful window displays that always captivated the occupants of cars as they waited by the traffic lights. Each window was carefully colour coordinated – blue and lilac in one, perhaps, and yellow and white in another. Constantly changing, the new colour schemes of the displays were always a surprise and a delight. Elizabeth's is now Henry's Coffee Shop. There are still delights to behold through the windows, but now it is a frothy cappuccino or buttered scone that captivates the passer-by. The Old Rock Shop Bistro has also replaced a fondly remembered Cromer shop. A traditional seaside rock shop used to be on the site and it sold, among other wares, full English breakfasts made completely of peppermint rock. The café that took over the building still sells a full breakfast, but with a somewhat different flavour.

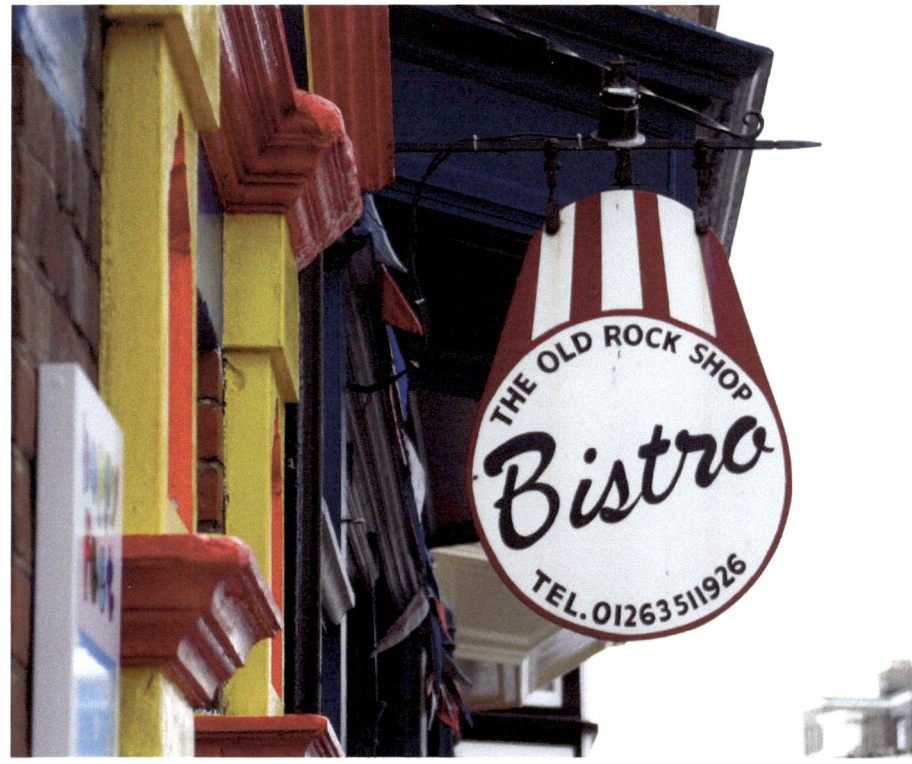
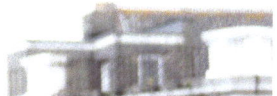

Modern establishments have preserved elements of old-fashioned charm.

About with Friends is a community café in Cromer staffed by people with learning difficulties. The cafe benefits its staff by helping them to learn skills for the future. The site that About with Friends occupies is steeped in the past. It used to be The Blue Danube café. The Blue Danube first started trading nearly a century ago in North Lodge Park. It was elegant, very continental and even had a fig tree growing up to a glass roof. The fig tree was extremely useful during the Second World War. It fruited well and meant that the Women's Institute could make their traditional Christmas puddings for the disadvantaged in the town, at a time when rationing was in place. There were plans during wartime to further help the disadvantaged by turning the Blue Danube into a British Restaurant. British Restaurants were canteens provided by the ministry of food to give a cheap, nutritionally balanced meal to those who were struggling to make ends meet, often due to running out of food coupons and having no rations. The plan did not go ahead in the end, but the manager may have been struggling to make ends meet herself during rationing, as she was prosecuted and fined £3 by the magistrates' court for procuring 4 gallons of black-market milk. This was not the only café to be fined during the Second World War: the Orange Tree Cafe's manager was fined £2 for allowing a flashing display to be seen. The magistrate commented that, 'Advertising was important but not as important as the blackout.' The Blue Danube later moved to the site now occupied by About with Friends and was painted to look like the genuine Viennese coffee shop that its name implied. Residents and tourists still remember the Blue Danube as being the place

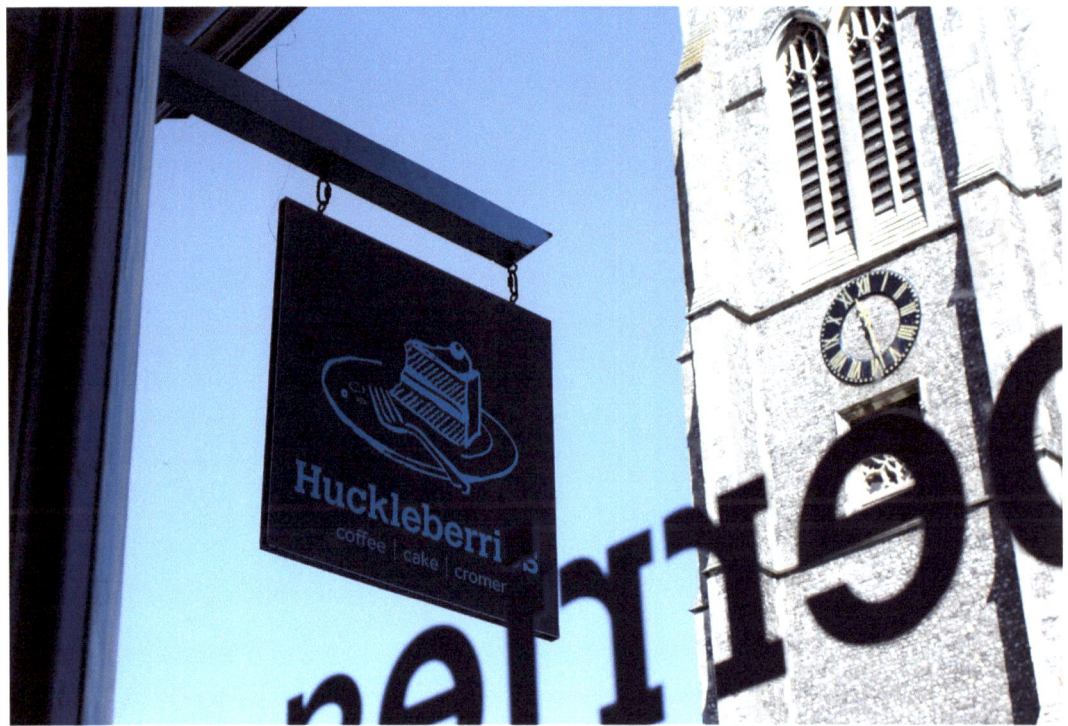

Many different cafés have looked out over Cromer church.

they had their first hot chocolate, served in a tall mug and topped with a mountain of whipped cream – they would wrap their hands around it and watch the revolving display of gateaux while the rain beat down outside.

The Rocket House Café also has a long history. The Cromer café is so-called because the lifeboat station that was previously on the site was a base for firing rockets to distressed ships at sea, the only way to get the lifesaving Manbys apparatus out to them. The first café on the site was the Rocket House Gardens. Created in the 1930s, it stood on the cliff behind the present café in an area of sunken gardens. The building was destroyed in a Second World War bombing raid. It was rebuilt, only to need rebuilding again after the flood tide of 1953 washed it away. The present café is new and has a very contemporary design. However, the modernity of the Rocket House still fits in well with the charm of Cromer seafront.

In Sheringham, the Whelk Coppers is a popular and pretty café overlooking the sea. The wrought-iron gates at the front of the building, with their underwater motif, were designed by the friend of a former owner. This friend was said to be none other than Walt Disney, who created a little piece of Disney Land on the Norfolk coast.

Some cafés are the elegant venue for afternoon tea or the place to get an expertly crafted latte. Others are perfect to get a mug of builder's tea to accompany another tradition of

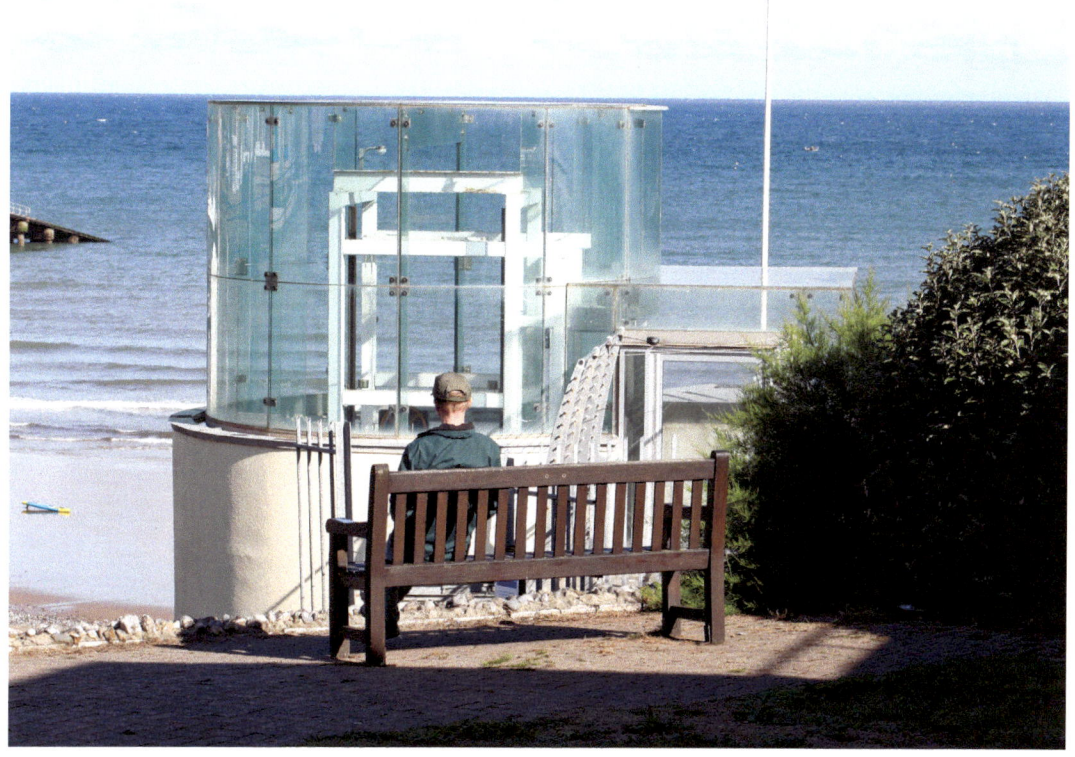

The modern Rocket House café commands a wonderful view.

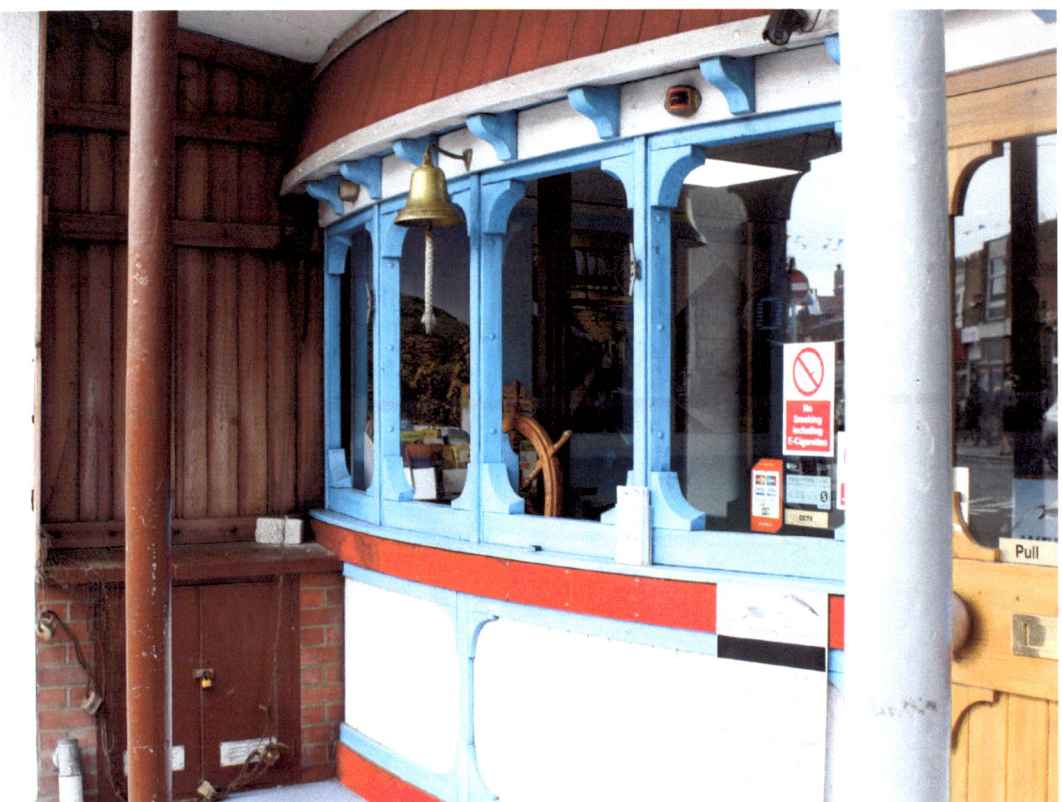

Some fish and chip cafés actually look like fishing boats.

the seaside: fish and chips. Celebrating this tradition, The Sheringham Trawler is a fish and chip shop with a front shaped like a fishing boat and it is said to be the best place for fish and chips in the town. In Cromer, Mary Jane's claims that distinction and the café and takeaway there has been trading for well over fifty years.

Fish and chips shops are found everywhere in the country but there is something about the scent of vinegary chips and the salty sea air that means a trip to Cromer and Sheringham wouldn't be the same without enjoying some. The origins of fish and chips lie in both the industrial cities of northern England and the East End of London. A Mr Lees of Oldham claims to have sold the first fish and chips in the 1860s; however, this honour is also claimed by a Mr Malin who opened his fish and chip shop in London's East End around the same time. Charles Dickens mentions the street selling of fried fish in *Oliver Twist*, and as this was written in 1839, it is likely that the fish part of the meal originated in London. Deep fried slices of potato had a background in Ireland but came over to England during the early nineteenth century. The first chips were sold to Irish dockers in the port of Liverpool, and the popularity spread to become a cheap and filling food for factory workers in the industrial towns of the North. Whether it was Mr Lees or Mr Malin who decided to put these two foods together and open the first fish and chip shop may never be proved, but their legacy remains.

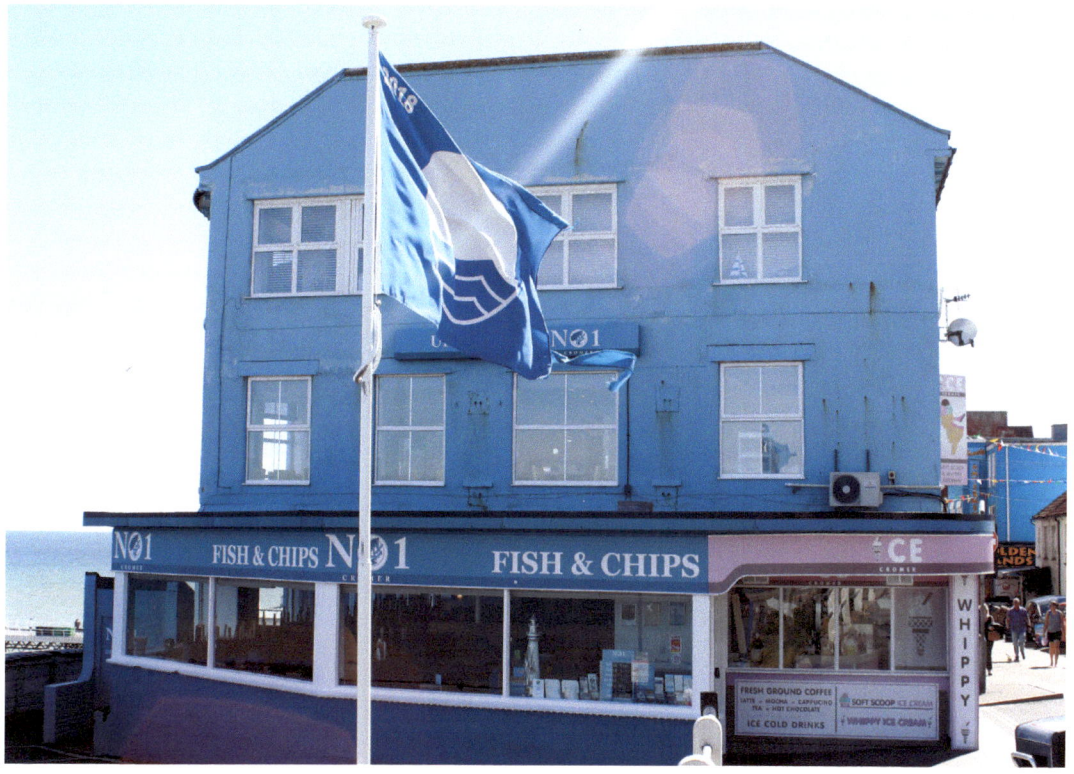

Fish and chips are a staple part of seaside cuisine.

DID YOU KNOW?
A speciality of Cromer cafés is crab. Dressed crab is a very British way to serve it and Cromer crab is reputed to be the best. However, there are many interesting things to know about brown crabs, other than how to cook them. Their lifespan is about thirty years but crabs are known to reach their centenary. Not all their time is spent walking sideways as a crab can walk in any direction, just not as fast. A crab's teeth are not in their mouths but, surprisingly, in their stomachs, and, finally, male crabs are called cocks, and females called hens.

The availability of fresh fish in Cromer and Sheringham meant that cafés all over the towns started to serve fish and chips. Holidaymakers from all levels of society became drawn to a meal that was cooked by someone else, and also instantly available. Fish and chips did not go on ration during the Second World War and it became the staple dish that many cafés in the towns served to the numerous military personnel. Each vendor had their own unique cooking style and recipe. The market continued to grow in the post-war years, when a new wave of working-class tourists started to arrive in Cromer and Sheringham following the introduction of paid annual leave. Fish and chips were ideal to provide the inexpensive catering they required. Many more cafés, and especially takeaways, were opened to meet their needs.

Cafés, coffee shops and pubs are now the backbone of Cromer and Sheringham high streets. However, the lines of distinction between the different kinds of venue have become a little blurred with the passing of time. Bars and pubs now serve the tea, coffee and full English breakfasts that used to be the preserve of the café, and some cafés are licensed for alcohol. Coffee shops have become a place to sit and chat over a drink or two and most pubs readily welcome children. There is a risk that all establishments will merge and become faceless. Not so in Cromer and Sheringham. Here, everyone remembers the cafés. Sometimes it is with a nostalgic thought, sometimes it is as a means of identifying a location and sometimes it is just because a particular café is the best place to go for a cup of tea. The changing face of the high streets and their various cafés, tells the story of Cromer and Sheringham as much as anything else from the towns' history. There are hidden pasts, surprising facts and secrets behind every façade. If you could ask a visitor from any era of Cromer and Sheringham's tourist past what it is about the towns they remember best, they would just smile and say, 'Ah yes, that's where that lovely café is!'

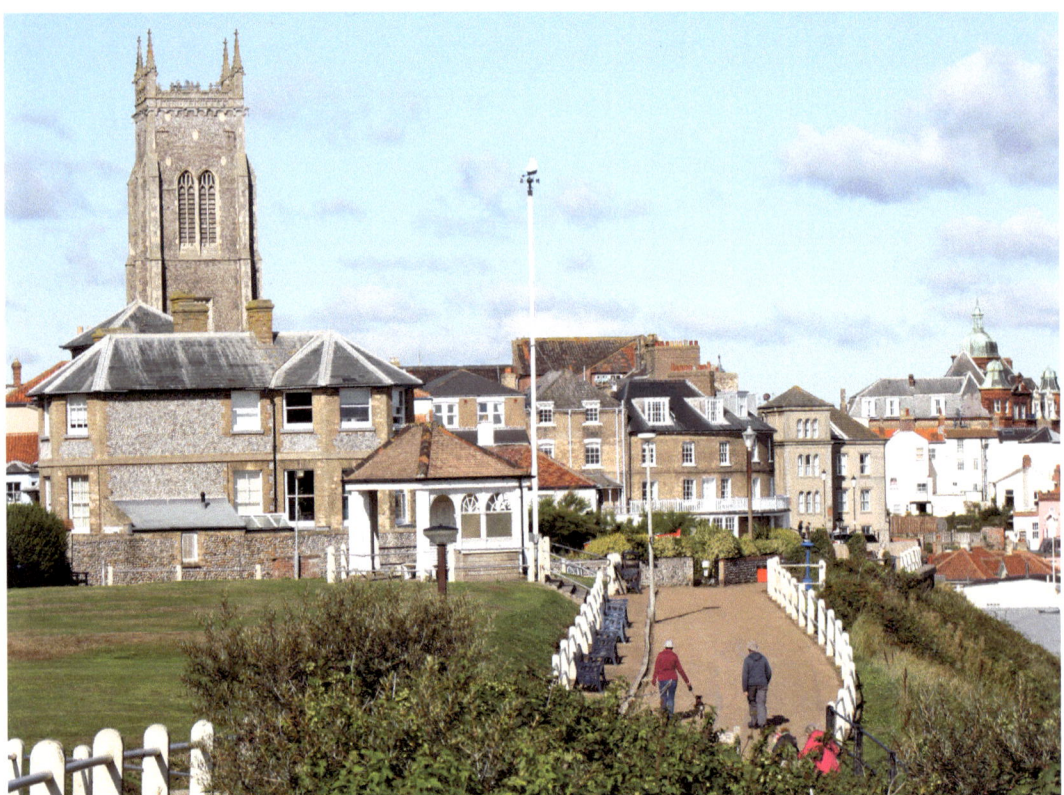

Sheringham and Cromer have busy cafés to refresh their visitors.

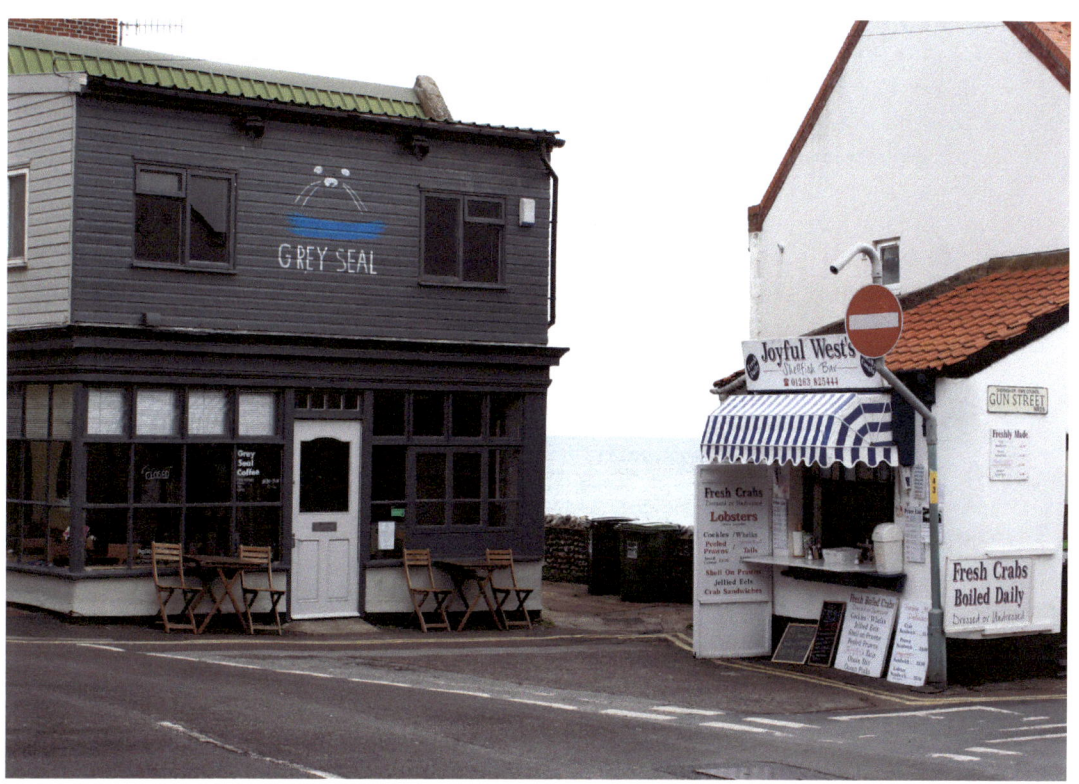

Fine coffee, good food and a view is always remembered.

Bibliography

Brooks, P., *Coastal Towns at War* (Poppyland Publishing, 1988)

Brooks, P., *Sheringham: The Story of a Town* (Poppyland Publishing, 2013)

Pipe, C., *A Dictionary of Cromer and Overstrand History* (Poppyland Publishing, 2010)

Pipe, C., *The Story of Cromer Pier* (Poppyland Publishing, 1998)

Rouse, M., *Cromer and Sheringham Through Time* (Amberly Publishing, 2010)